Unveiling the Mystique: Diversity in Geography of North-East India

Volume – II

Edited by:

Sailajananda Saikia
Department of Geography, Rajiv Gandhi University, Rono Hills – Doimukh, Papum Pare – 791112, Arunachal Pradesh, India.
E-mail: sailajananda.saikia@rgu.ac.in

Gibji Nimasow
Department of Geography, Rajiv Gandhi University, Rono Hills – Doimukh, Papum Pare – 791112, Arunachal Pradesh, India.
E-mail: gibji.nimasow@rgu.ac.in

Tage Rupa Sora
Department of Geography, Rajiv Gandhi University, Rono Hills – Doimukh, Papum Pare – 791112, Arunachal Pradesh, India.
E-mail: tage.rupa@rgu.ac.in

<u>PREFACE</u>

With its diverse cultures, landscapes, and customs, India's northeastern area occupies a special place in the subcontinent's geographical and cultural diversity. Arunachal Pradesh and Assam are two of its eight sister states that stand out for their dynamic communities, rich history, and stunning natural beauty. Unveiling the Mystique: Diversity in Geography of North East India is a book that aims to provide insights into the socioeconomic realities, cultural legacy, and environmental challenges of this region while also exploring its many facets.

This book uses a combination of current scientific methods and traditional knowledge to explore a different facet of the geography of the area in each of its chapters. From the study of soil erosion in Assam's Dibrugarh District to the discovery of water storage sites in Arunachal Pradesh using cutting-edge geospatial techniques, the research presented here covers a wide range of issues. The chapters also examine the socioeconomic effects of modern activities like oil palm agriculture on indigenous livelihoods and the ramifications of development initiatives like the rebirth of the old Stilwell Road.

The comprehension of the human-environment interaction in the area is a major focus of our effort. Examples of the close relationship between people and their environment include the examination of traditional *Nyishi* beads and jewelry, the research of traditional dress patterns in the *Apatani* group, and the analysis of solid waste management in the Itanagar Capital Region. These chapters show the continuous struggles and changes that these communities endure in addition to documenting the customs of the local culture.

This book's wide range of subjects, from the investigation of riverbank instability to the spread of COVID-19 in Assam, highlights the intricate interactions between human and natural forces that have shaped Northeast India's terrain. By providing insightful viewpoints for scholars, politicians, and anyone else interested in the sustainable development of this intriguing region of India, the study findings given here hope to advance knowledge of the geographical diversity of the area.

Unveiling the Mystique: Diversity in Geography of North East India is a celebration of the flexibility and resiliency of the people of Northeast India, not only an anthology of scholarly works. It is a voyage into a place where the past and present coexist in a precarious equilibrium and where each river, mountain, and valley has a story to tell. It is our goal that this book will stimulate more research into and understanding of the astonishing diversity that shapes the geography of this amazing region.

List of Contributors

Ahai Wangsu Department of Geography, Rajiv Gandhi University, Itanagar- 791112, Arunachal Pradesh, India	**Manngam Wangpan** Department of Geography, Rajiv Gandhi University, Itanagar- 791112, Arunachal Pradesh, India
Praduyt Dey Department of Geography, Rajiv Gandhi University, Itanagar- 791112, Arunachal Pradesh, India	**Habung Hagio** Department of Geography, Rajiv Gandhi University, Itanagar- 791112, Arunachal Pradesh, India
Ligang Aniya Department of Geography, Rajiv Gandhi University, Itanagar- 791112, Arunachal Pradesh, India	**Sagir Hussain** Department of Geography, Rajiv Gandhi University, Itanagar- 791112, Arunachal Pradesh, India
Rani Cheda Department of Geography, Rajiv Gandhi University, Itanagar- 791112, Arunachal Pradesh, India	**Duyu Nanya** Department of Geography, Rajiv Gandhi University, Itanagar- 791112, Arunachal Pradesh, India
Chitra Rani Barua	**Duyu Monya** Department of Fruit Science, College of Horticulture and Forestry, CAU (I) Pasighat- 791102, Arunachal Pradesh, India
Pumung Ngemu Department of Geography, Rajiv Gandhi University, Itanagar- 791112, Arunachal Pradesh, India	**Arpana Handique** Centre for Studies in Geography, Dibrugarh University, Dibrugarh, India
Dipak Sharma Department of Geography, Rajiv Gandhi University, Itanagar- 791112, Arunachal Pradesh, India	**Sailajananda Saikia** Department of Geography, Rajiv Gandhi University, Itanagar- 791112, Arunachal Pradesh, India
Santanu Kumar Patnaik Department of Geography, Rajiv Gandhi University, Itanagar- 791112, Arunachal Pradesh, India	**Nishamani Kar** Department of Geography, Rajiv Gandhi University, Itanagar- 791112, Arunachal Pradesh, India
Tage Rupa Sora Department of Geography, Rajiv Gandhi University, Itanagar- 791112, Arunachal Pradesh, India	**Latifa Ara Khanam** Department of Geography, Rajiv Gandhi University, Itanagar- 791112, Arunachal Pradesh, India
Parishmita Hazarika Department of Geography, Rajiv Gandhi University, Itanagar- 791112, Arunachal Pradesh, India	**Naitik Kumar Biswas** Department of Geography, Rajiv Gandhi University, Itanagar- 791112, Arunachal Pradesh, India

TABLE OF CONTENTS

Preface

List of Contributors

CHAPTER 1

Identification of Surface Water Storage Sites of Longding District, Arunachal Pradesh using Topographic Wetness Index (TWI) and Normalized Difference Vegetation Index (NDVI)

Ahai Wangsu[1] and Santanu Kumar Patnaik[2]

Abstract

Water is one of the most important elements needed to sustain life on earth. Identification and analysis of surface water resources are essential to ensuring proper management and planning of the available resources so as to ensure optimal utilization and sustainability. The study has been done to identify the potential surface water storage sites in Longding District in Arunachal Pradesh. In this study, TWI and NDVI have been used to identify the locations suitable for surface water harvesting using GIS. TWI was prepared using the ALOSPALSAR Digital Elevation Model (DEM). NDVI has been prepared using Sentinel 2 imagery. The indices have been used for the identification of water storage sites. Overlays of the generated maps were done using a raster calculator in the ArcGIS environment. Areas with high TWI values indicate low-lying areas were found to have high water accumulation potential, and vice versa. The NDVI class of water bodies was found to be the best suitable sites for water harvesting. The areas marked by the combination of high TWI and water bodies of NDVI were found to be zones with the highest potential for surface water harvesting. The derived maps were then validated through field surveys. It was found that the computed TWI and NDVI maps correspond with ground reality and thus can be used for the identification of suitable sites for water harvesting.

Keywords: GIS, NDVI, TWI, Water Harvesting Zone.

Introduction:

The surface water body has an irreplaceable role in the global ecology and climate system (Donchyts et al., 2016; Jiang et al., 2020; Pekel et al., 2016). Therefore, accurate monitoring of surface water is of great significance to hydrological processes and water resource management (Donchyts et al.,

2016). Surface water plays an important role in the climate system and the hydrological cycle. Proper monitoring and delineation of the surface water bodies has a crucial role in resource management. Water insecurity and scarcity are two of the most pressing issues that the world as a whole is facing. With an increasing population and rising demand for water to sustain life, the available water resources are strained, leading to water scarcity. Water harvesting can act as insurance in periods of water shortage and scarcity. Patterns of rainfall have been changing with global climate change. As such, there is erratic rainfall, with wet and dry spells intermittently. Advancements in GIS and Remote Sensing techniques have made it easier to assess hydrological processes at the local, regional, and global levels. Spatial and temporal features of watersheds can be derived and analyzed using GIS and Remote Sensing.

The study area is characterized by high rainfall conditions during the monsoon months from June to September. The winter months from November to February are marked by dry conditions. It is during these months that the area faces an acute shortage of water. Surface water harvesting can be adopted as an important technique for supplying water for drinking and domestic purposes during periods of water crisis during the winter months. Successful water harvesting can be adopted after identifying suitable sites for water storage. Water harvesting during the high precipitation periods can act as a buffer to meet the needs during the water crisis period and also make use of the surplus water that would otherwise run-off. It can be used as a measure to meet the demands for drinking and domestic purposes, thereby relieving the excess pressure on the other surface water sources in the study area, such as rivers, streams, ponds, springs, etc. Identification of potential water storage sites is important to ensure successful planning and adaptation of surface water harvesting.

Study Area:

The study has been carried out in the Longding District of Arunachal Pradesh. The practice of shifting cultivation on a large scale has resulted in the reckless cutting of forests and deforestation in the area. The climate of the district is directly related to the terrain, where areas of high elevation experience a cold and humid climate. The monsoon season is marked by heavy rainfall, which occurs during the months from June to September. The winter months from November to February are marked by cold and dry weather. The vegetation comprises tropical, subtropical, and temperate forests, which are directly related to the variability in rainfall and elevation. The slope of the study area has been calculated in terms of degrees. It has been classified into four classes: flat slopes ranging between 0-10 degrees, gentle slopes between 0-21 degrees, moderately steep slopes between 21-31 degrees, and steep slope areas ranging between 31-42 degrees. It was found that 52% of the total area of the district is covered by gentle slopes, followed by flat, moderately steep, and steep slope areas. The elevation zones have been divided into five classes: 58-554 m, 554-1051 m, 1051-1547 m, 1547-2044 m, and 2044-2541 m. The altitude or height of the area is proportionally related to the water storage capacity of the region. Steep slopes are characteristic of high surface run-off, while low-lying areas are marked by high water holding or storing capacity.

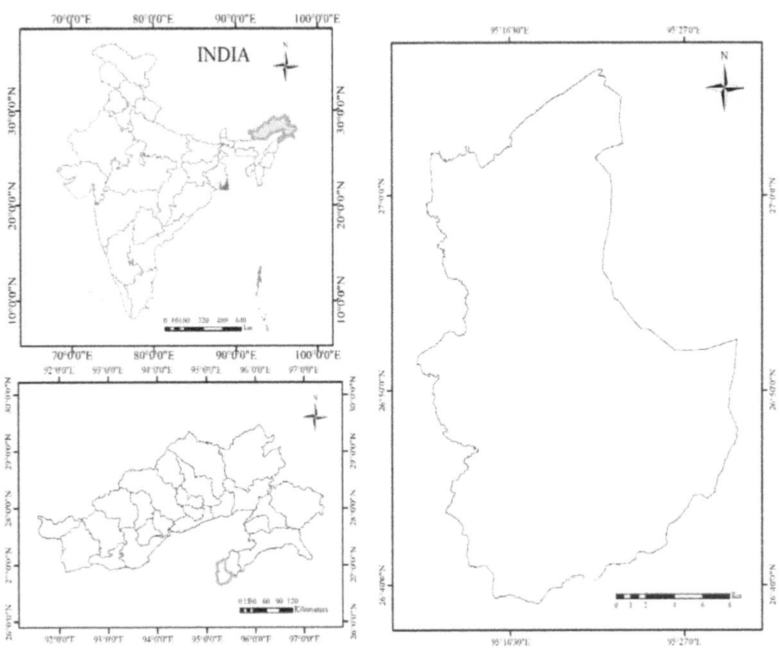

Fig. 1: - Location map of the Study Area

Dataset:

GIS has been used to generate the required maps. ALOS PALSAR DEM with a resolution of 12.5 metres was downloaded from the USGS Earth Explorer. DEM was used to generate the Topographic Wetness Index (TWI) of the study area. Sentinel 2 imagery was downloaded from USGS Earth Explorer. It has a resolution of 10 metres. The Normalized Difference Vegetation Index (NDVI) was generated using the Sentinel 2 data.

Methodology:

The Topographic Wetness Index (TWI) is widely used in environmental and ecological studies (Piedallu et al., 2019; Schmitt et al., 2020). TWI was developed by Beven and Kirby in 1979. In the TWI, the slope gradient approximates down slope water drainage, and the specific catchment area, calculated as the total catchment area divided by the flow width, approximates the water supply from the upslope area (Beven and Kirkby, 1979). It is a function of slope and the upstream contributing area per unit width to the flow direction. The index is associated with different soil attributes and soil characteristics. TWI calculates the accumulation of moisture from the upslope water catchment area and the low-lying down slope area for each cell in a DEM. TWI can be used to study the spatial scale effects on the hydrological cycle. Availability of high resolution DEMs has increased the scope and accuracy of TWI calculation. TWI is defined as:

ln a / tan b

Where **a** is the local upslope area draining through a certain point per unit contour length, and **tan b** is the local slope in radians.

NDVI is a numerical indicator that uses the visible and near-infrared bands of the electromagnetic spectrum. Vegetation will have positive values and water will tend to have negative values. $NDVI_i$ represents smoothed NDVI (sNDVI) observed at time step and their ratio yields a measure of photosynthetic activity within values between − 1 and 1. Its values are negative for water bodies, close to zero for rocks, sands, or concrete surfaces, and positive for vegetation, including crops, shrubs, grasses, and forests (Jones and Vaughan. 2010). Low NDVI values indicate moisture-stressed vegetation and higher values indicate a higher density of green vegetation. It is also used for drought monitoring and famine early warning (Wardlow et al., 2007; Javadnia et al., 2009). NDVI can be used for delineating the different vegetation and vegetation stress. It is one of the most used indexes used for vegetation studies owing to its simplicity which can be obtained using the available spectral images. It is expressed as: **NDVI = (Near Infrared − Red) / (Near Infrared + Red)**

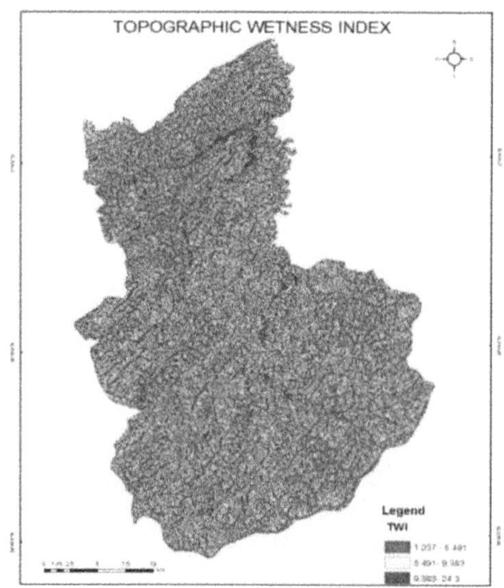

Fig.2:- TWI map of Longding District, Arunachal Pradesh

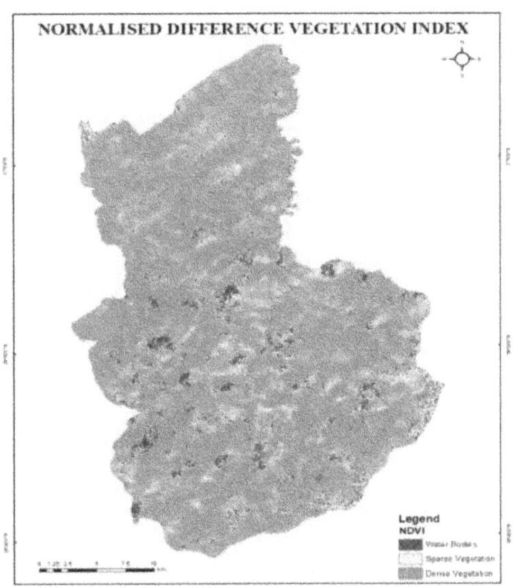

Fig.3:- NDVI map of Longding District, Arunachal Pradesh

Overlay analysis was carried out in ArcGIS using raster calculator to derive the suitable sites for identification of potential surface water storage sites.

Results and Discussions:

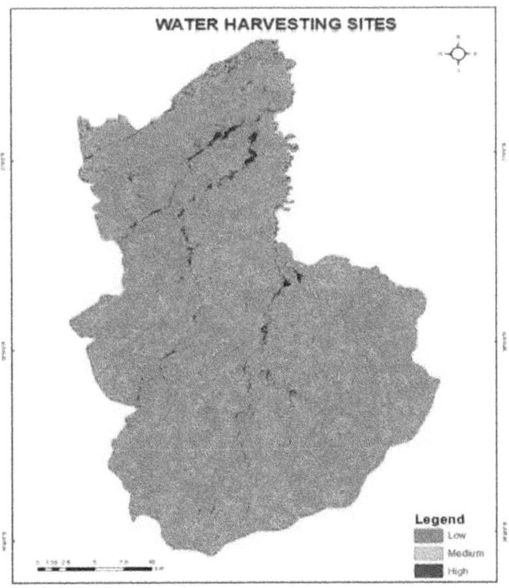

Fig. 4:- Potential Water Harvesting Sites of Longding District, Arunachal Pradesh

High TWI values indicate higher flow accumulation which is found in the relatively low-lying areas as it has higher water holding capacity. Smaller values indicate high run-off condition marked by steep areas. The computed TWI has range between 1.237 to 24.318. The study area was classified into three different classes with TWI values as low, medium and high water accumulation regions. High values indicate the low-lying region with higher water storing capacity and low slope condition. The computed TWI is given in Fig.2.

NDVI values were classified into three categories to identify water bodies and dry lands. Upon using a threshold value to classify the two, it has been found that the NDVI values provide correct values for identifying the two different classes. The NDVI have values between -0.123 to 1. Negative values indicate water bodies. The study area was categorized into dense vegetation, sparse vegetation and water bodies for identification of potential water storage sites.

Identification and selection of potential locations for surface water harvesting was carried out based on the TWI and NDVI maps. The ideal locations were selected based on the high TWI values which are equivalent to higher water concentration areas. The NDVI class of water bodies was found to be suitable for water harvesting sites as compared to the sparse and dense vegetation class. Overlay in Arc GIS was used for joining the two indices to provide a single output for selection of suitable water storage sites. The study area was classified into three different classes based on the output as areas with low water storage capacity, medium storage capacity and high-water storage capacity sites. The map has been given in Fig. 4. According to the classification high water storage capacity sites are those with TWI values ranging between 9.383 to 24.318 and NDVI class of "water bodies". The least suitable area for water harvesting is the ones with the combination of low TWI values between 1.237 to 5.491 of low water accumulation zones with steep slopes and NDVI value of "sparse vegetation".

Advancements in remote sensing and GIS techniques have made it a lot easier for identification and selection of locations with different potential for planning and implementation. The use of GIS, satellite imagery and DEM for identification of pater storage sites were found to be cost effective and can be used to supplement in solving the problem of water shortage and crisis with high accuracy levels.

References:

Aguilar, C., Zinnert, J. C., Polo, M. J., & Young, D. R. (2012). NDVI as an indicator for changes in water availability to woody vegetation. *Ecological Indicators*, *23*, 290–300. https://doi.org/10.1016/j.ecolind.2012.04.008

Anderson, J. R., Hardy, E. E., Roach, J. T., & Witmer, R. E. (1976). A land use and land cover classification system for use with remote sensor data. *U.S. Geological Survey Professional Papers/U.S. Geological Survey Professional Paper*. https://doi.org/10.3133/pp964

Band, L. E., Hwang, T., Hales, T., Vose, J., & Ford, C. (2012). Ecosystem processes at the watershed scale: Mapping and modeling ecohydrological controls of landslides. *Geomorphology*, *137*(1), 159–167. https://doi.org/10.1016/j.geomorph.2011.06.025

Berhanu, B., & Bisrat, E. (2018). Identification of surface water storing sites using Topographic Wetness Index (TWI) and Normalized Difference Vegetation Index (NDVI). *Journal of Natural Resources and Development*, *8*, 91–100. https://doi.org/10.5027/jnrd.v8i0.09

Beven, K. J., & Kirkby, M. J. (1979). A physically based, variable contributing area model of basin hydrology / Un modèle à base physique de zone d'appel variable de l'hydrologie du bassin versant. *Hydrological Sciences Bulletin*, *24*(1), 43–69. https://doi.org/10.1080/02626667909491834

Bhangale, U., More, S., Shaikh, T., Patil, S., & More, N. (2020). Analysis of surface water resources using Sentinel-2 imagery. *Procedia Computer Science*, *171*, 2645–2654. https://doi.org/10.1016/j.procs.2020.04.287

Buchanan, B. P., Fleming, M., Schneider, R. L., Richards, B. K., Archibald, J., Qiu, Z., & Walter, M. T. (2014). Evaluating topographic wetness indices across central New York agricultural landscapes. *Hydrology and Earth System Sciences*, *18*(8), 3279–3299. https://doi.org/10.5194/hess-18-3279-2014

Donchyts, G., Schellekens, J., Winsemius, H., Eisemann, E., & Van De Giesen, N. (2016). A 30 m Resolution Surface Water Mask Including Estimation of Positional and Thematic Differences Using Landsat 8, SRTM and OpenStreetMap: A Case Study in the Murray-Darling Basin, Australia. *Remote Sensing*, *8*(5), 386. https://doi.org/10.3390/rs8050386

Gleick, P. H. (2000). A look at twenty-first century water resources development. *Water International*, *25*(1), 127–138. https://doi.org/10.1080/02508060008686804

Grabs, T., Seibert, J., Bishop, K., & Laudon, H. (2009). Modelling spatial patterns of saturated areas: A comparison of the topographic wetness index and a dynamic distributed model. *Journal of Hydrology*, *373*(1–2), 15–23. https://doi.org/10.1016/j.jhydrol.2009.03.031

Leh, M. D., & Chaubey, I. (2009). GIS-Based Predictive Models of Hillslope Runoff Generation Processes1. *Journal of the American Water Resources Association*, *45*(4), 844–856. https://doi.org/10.1111/j.1752-1688.2009.00328.x

Mattivi, P., Franci, F., Lambertini, A., & Bitelli, G. (2019). TWI computation: a comparison of different open-source GISs. *Open Geospatial Data, Software and Standards*, *4*(1). https://doi.org/10.1186/s40965-019-0066-y

Mays, L. W. (2009). *Integrated urban water management: arid and semi-arid regions.* https://ci.nii.ac.jp/ncid/BB01356355

Murphy, P. N., Ogilvie, J., Meng, F., White, B., Bhatti, J. S., & Arp, P. A. (2011). Modelling and mapping topographic variations in forest soils at high resolution: A case study. *Ecological Modelling*, *222*(14), 2314–2332. https://doi.org/10.1016/j.ecolmodel.2011.01.003

Özelkan, E. (2020). Water Body Detection Analysis Using NDWI Indices Derived from Landsat-8 OLI. *Polish Journal of Environmental Studies*, *29*(2), 1759–1769. https://doi.org/10.15244/pjoes/110447

Payen, J., Faurès, J., &Vallée, D. (2019). Small reservoirs and water storage for smallholder farming--the case for a new approach. *Gates Open Res*, *3*, 387. https://doi.org/10.21955/gatesopenres.1115486.1

Qin, C., Zhu, A., Pei, T., Li, B., Scholten, T., Behrens, T., & Zhou, C. (2009). An approach to computing topographic wetness index based on maximum downslope gradient. *Precision Agriculture*, *12*(1), 32–43. https://doi.org/10.1007/s11119-009-9152-y

Rokni, K., Ahmad, A., Selamat, A., &Hazini, S. (2014). Water feature extraction and change detection using multitemporal landsat imagery. *Remote Sensing*, *6*(5), 4173–4189. https://doi.org/10.3390/rs6054173

Różycka, M., Migoń, P., & Michniewicz, A. (2017). Topographic Wetness Index and Terrain Ruggedness Index in geomorphic characterisation of landslide terrains, on examples from the

Sudetes, SW Poland. *Zeitschrift Für Geomorphologie*, *61*(2), 61–80. https://doi.org/10.1127/zfg_suppl/2016/0328

Ruhoff, A. L., Castro, N. M. R., & Risso, A. (2011). Numerical Modelling of the Topographic Wetness Index: An analysis at different scales. *International Journal of Geosciences*, *02*(04), 476–483. https://doi.org/10.4236/ijg.2011.24050

Stieglitz, M., Shaman, J., McNamara, J., Engel, V., Shanley, J., & Kling, G. W. (2003). An approach to understanding hydrologic connectivity on the hillslope and the implications for nutrient transport. *Global Biogeochemical Cycles*, *17*(4). https://doi.org/10.1029/2003gb002041

Water harvesting in Sub-Saharan Africa. (2013). In *Routledge eBooks*. https://doi.org/10.4324/9780203109984

CHAPTER 2

Modeling and Estimation of Soil Erosion in the Dibrugarh District, Assam using Revised Universal Soil Loss Equation (RUSLE)

Praduyt Dey, Arpana Handique, and Santanu Kumar Patnaik

Abstract

Soil erosion is a critical global challenge, resulting in the loss of fertile topsoil and contributing to decreased agricultural productivity, increased sedimentation in waterways, and ecosystem disruption. It is an emerging threat to sustainable land management in Dibrugarh District, Assam. This study uses the Revised Universal Soil Loss Equation (RUSLE) model, integrated with remote sensing and GIS, to quantify soil erosion. Results show that 91.147% of the area experiences very slight erosion (<2 t ha-1 yr-1), while severe erosion affects 0.148% and very severe erosion impacts 0.044% of the area, requiring urgent conservation efforts. Effective soil management and targeted conservation strategies are essential to mitigate erosion and ensure long-term land productivity and environmental health in the region.

Keywords: Soil erosion, Remote sensing and GIS, RUSLE, soil management

Introduction:

Soil erosion, a critical environmental issue, involves the detachment, transport, and deposition of soil particles, leading to the degradation of the topsoil layer (Jazouli et al. 2017). This natural process is exacerbated by various anthropogenic activities, including deforestation, overgrazing, construction, and mining (Jayasekara et al. 2018). The significance of soil erosion extends beyond the loss of fertile soil, as it impacts water quality, agricultural productivity, and ecosystem stability (Ayalew et al. 2020).

In recent years, the research community has focused on quantifying soil erosion and sediment yield in river basins using remote sensing and GIS techniques (Benavidez et al. 2018; Sarma et al. 2021; Negese et al. 2021; Handique et al. 2023). Traditional methods of soil erosion assessment are often time-consuming and costly, especially for large study areas such as district blocks. In this context, modeling aided by remote sensing and GIS provides valuable insights into current erosion processes and facilitates future predictions.

The Universal Soil Loss Equation (USLE), developed by Wischmeier and Smith in 1968, revolutionized soil erosion prediction from cropland. This model gained worldwide popularity for its simplicity and effectiveness. In the early 1990s, the USLE model was updated and computerized, resulting in the Revised Universal Soil Loss Equation (RUSLE). This updated model integrates remote sensing and GIS, offering a robust tool for predicting average annual soil erosion rates based on rainfall, soil, topography, cropping systems, and soil management practices (Wijesundara et al. 2018).

The RUSLE model considers several factors: rainfall erosivity (R), soil erodibility (K), topography (LS), cover and management (C), and support practices (P). These factors collectively contribute to a comprehensive understanding of soil erosion dynamics in a given area.

This study aims to estimate soil erosion in the Dibrugarh district using the RUSLE model integrated with remote sensing and GIS techniques. By analyzing the spatial distribution of soil erosion severity, this research seeks to provide critical insights for effective soil conservation and sustainable land management practices in the region.

Study Area:

Dibrugarh is situated between 27°5'38" to 27°42'03" N latitude and 94°33'46" E to 95°29'08" E longitude in Assam, spanning an area of approximately 3381 sq. km (Fig. 1). It is located in the northeastern segment of the upper Brahmaputra valley. The Dhemaji and Lakhimpur districts border it towards the north, while the Tirap district of Arunachal Pradesh lies to the south. Tinsukia and Sivasagar districts are located to its east and west, respectively. Geographically, the area displays diverse features, including vast floodplains, swamps, wetlands, and occasional hills. The Brahmaputra River runs along the district's northern edge, and the BurhiDihing River, a significant tributary of the Brahmaputra, with its extensive network of tributaries and wetlands (beels), flows through the region. Dibrugarh district in Assam has a humid subtropical climate, characterized by intensely rainy summers and relatively dry winters (Bora et al. 2023).

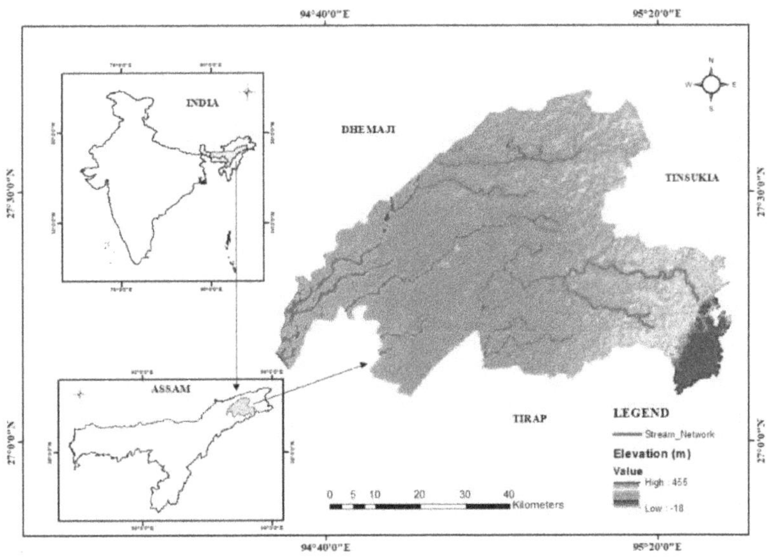

Fig. 1:- Location of the study area.

Materials and Methods:

Data Collection-

The study utilized multiple geospatial datasets sourced from various repositories. The datasets included rainfall data, soil information, digital elevation model (DEM), and satellite imagery, all essential for the RUSLE model implementation. A cloud-free Landsat 8 OLI satellite image was obtained from the United States Geological Survey (USGS) on 20th December 2023 to derive land cover and management details. Additionally, a 30-meter resolution SRTM 1 Arc-Second DEM, acquired on 21 December 2023, was used to assess topographical impacts on soil erosion. The DEM dataset was retrieved from Earth Explorer, managed by the United States Geological Survey (USGS).For rainfall analysis, the study employed high-resolution gridded average annual rainfall data (2021-22) acquired from the Climatic Research Unit (CRU) on 21 December 2023.Furthermore, standardized soil profile data, which provides detailed information on soil properties such as sand, silt, clay content, and organic carbon, was essential for analyzing soil erodibility. This data was acquired from the United States Food and Agriculture Organization (FAO) soil data portal. Fig. 2 shows the methodological flow chart of the entire research.

Application of RUSLE Model:

The RUSLE model estimates average annual soil loss (A) using five factors: rainfall erosivity (R), soil erodibility (K), slope length and steepness (LS), cover management (C), and conservation practices (P)(Renard et al. 1997), expressed as:

$$A = R \times K \times L \times S \times C \times P \tag{1}$$

Where, A = average annual soil loss (t ha−1 yr−1), R = rainfall erosivity factor (MJ mm ha−1 h −1, yr−1), K = soil erodibility factor (t h MJ−1 mm−1), LS = slope-length and slope steepness factor (dimensionless), C = land management factor (dimensionless), and P = conservation practice factor (dimensionless).

Computation of causative factors:

Rainfall Erosivity Factor (R)-

The R factor quantifies the erosive power of rainfall, measured in MJ mm ha^{-1} h^{-1} yr^{-1}. Due to data limitations, the empirical equation by Singh (1981) favorable for the Indian context was used:

$$R = 79 + 0.363\ AAP \tag{2}$$

Where 'AAP' is the average annual precipitation in mm. A rainfall map was generated using gridded rainfall data (1921-2022) and IDW interpolation techniques in ArcGIS 10.8.

Soil Erodibility Factor (K)-

The K factor measures soil loss per rainfall erosion index unit, influenced by soil texture, structure, organic matter, and porosity. Using soil data from the FAO, and extracting it with the area of interest (AOI), K values were calculated with the formula from Sharpley & Williams (1990):

$$K = Fcsand \times Fsi - cl \times Forgc \times Fhisand \times 0.1317 \tag{3}$$

$$Fcsand = \left[0.2 + 0.3.\exp\left(-0.256.SAN\left(1 - \frac{SIL}{100}\right)\right)\right] \tag{4}$$

$$Fsi - cl = \left[\frac{SIL}{CLA+SIL}\right]^{0.3} \tag{5}$$

$$Forgc = \left[1.0 - \frac{0.25\ C}{C+\exp(3.72-2.95C)}\right] \tag{6}$$

$$Fhisand = \left[1.0 - \frac{0.70\ SN_1}{SN_1+\exp(-5.51+2.95\ SN_1)}\right] \tag{7}$$

Where SAN, SIL, and CLA represent the percentages of sand, silt, and clay, respectively; C is the organic carbon content. SN1 is derived from the sand content by subtracting it from 1 and dividing by 100. Fcsand indicates a low soil erodibility factor for soils with coarse sand and a high factor for soils with low sand content. Fsi-cl reflects a low soil erodibility factor with a high clay-to-silt ratio. Forgc reduces soil erodibility for soils with high organic content, while Fhisand reduces soil erodibility for soils with extremely high sand content.

Slope Length and Steepness Factor (LS)-

The LS factor reflects terrain influence on soil erosion, calculated using SRTM DEM data and the Wischmeier & Smith (1957) equation:

$$\text{LS} = \left(\frac{\lambda}{\Psi}\right)^2 . (0.065 + 0.046s + 0.0065s^2) \tag{8}$$

where λ is flow path length, Ψ is 22.13 for SI units, and S is the average slope.

Cover and Management Factor (C) and Conservation Support Practice Factor (P)-

The C factor accounts for the impact of vegetation on soil erosion. A LULC map was created in ArcGIS 10.8, and C values were assigned based on land cover types (USDA-SCS, 1972; Wischmeier & Smith, 1978; Pandey et al. 2007).The P factor reflects conservation practices' effects on runoff and soil erosion, with values ranging from 0 (high conservation) to 1 (no conservation) (Wischmeier & Smith, 1957; Renard et al., 1997).

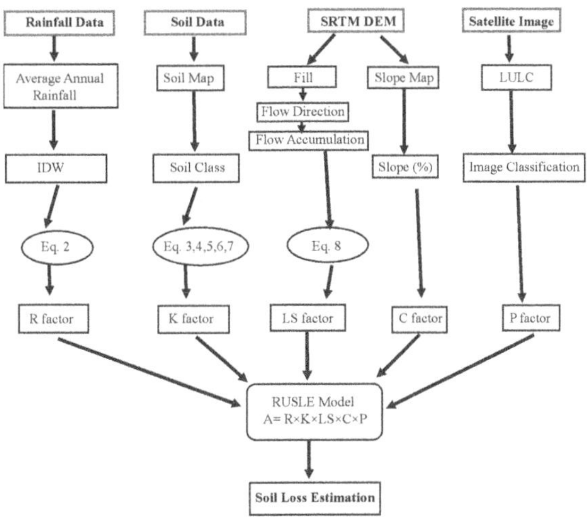

Fig. 2:- Flow chart of the methodological framework

Results and Discussions:

The soil erosion severity classes in the study for Dibrugarh district, Assam, were determined using the Revised Universal Soil Loss Equation (RUSLE) model. The RUSLE model used several factors to estimate soil erosion. The Rainfall erosivity factor (R) value was derived from the annual average rainfall of Dibrugarh district which ranges between 3971 and 4305 mm (Fig. 2. a). The R factor derived using eq. 2 ranges between 1520.54 to 1641.9 MJ mm ha^{-1} h^{-1} yr^{-1} (Fig. 2. b). The higher rainfall and K factor value was witnessed in the southeast and south-eastern portions of the region. Soil Erodibility Factor (K) is an important determinant of soil erosion derived from the study area's soil type map. The main soil categories found in the region are clay loam (Ao) covering 46.1 sq. km area (1.3%), sandy clay loam (Af) covering 2075.03 sq. km area (61.6%), and sandy clay loam (Ao) covering 1257.9 sq. km (37.3%) (Fig. 3 a). The K factor derived from eq. 3 (Table. 1) ranges between 0.018 to 0.020 h MJ^{-1} mm^{-1} (Fig. 3 b).

Table 1: Soil properties and the values of $f$csand, $f$cl-si, $f$orgC and $f$hisand and K factor

Classes	Area(sq. km)	Sand (%)	Silt (%)	Clay (%)	OC (%)	fcsand	forgc	fhisand	fsl si	K
Af48-2ab (A3637)	2075.03	61.7	14.4	23.9	0.91	0.2000004	0.993749	0.989864	0.745675	0.0193205
Ao79-a (3650)	1257.9	53.6	15.8	30.6	2.25	0.2000029	0.975001	0.998056	0.723839	0.0185534
Ao76-2/3c (4276)	46.1	46.1	21.6	27.4	1.73	0.2000108	0.977640	0.998867	0.782127	0.0201188

The influence of terrain and topography on soil erosion is represented by slope length (L) and slope steepness (S). The slope categories in the study area ranges between 0⁰ and 18.6⁰ which has been reclassed into five classes including, 0–2° covering 1833 sq. km (54.4%), 2 - 4° covering 875 sq. km (26%), 4 - 6° covering 343 sq. km (10.5%), 6 - 8° covering 152 sq. km (4.5%) and more than 8° covering 165 sq. km (4.8%) (Fig. 4. a). The LS factor generated using eq. 8 generated an LS factor map with value ranges between 0 to 18.64 (Fig 4. b). It was observed that when slope and flow accumulation increase, the LS factor also increases. The type of land cover and land use significantly affects a region's hydrologic components, including surface runoff, infiltration, and evapotranspiration. The LULC of the study area consists of river bodies covering 239.51 sq. km (7.1%), sand deposits covering 657.01 sq. km (19.5%), Forest area covering 238.74 sq. km (7.08%), agricultural land covering 967.31 sq. km (28.7%), plantation covering 731.8 sq. km (21.7%) and settlement and built-up area covering 545.54 sq. km (Fig. 5 a). The C and P factor values assigned to each LULC class are displayed in Table 2. The final C and P factor maps used in the estimation of soil erosion are shown in Fig. 5 b and 5 c.

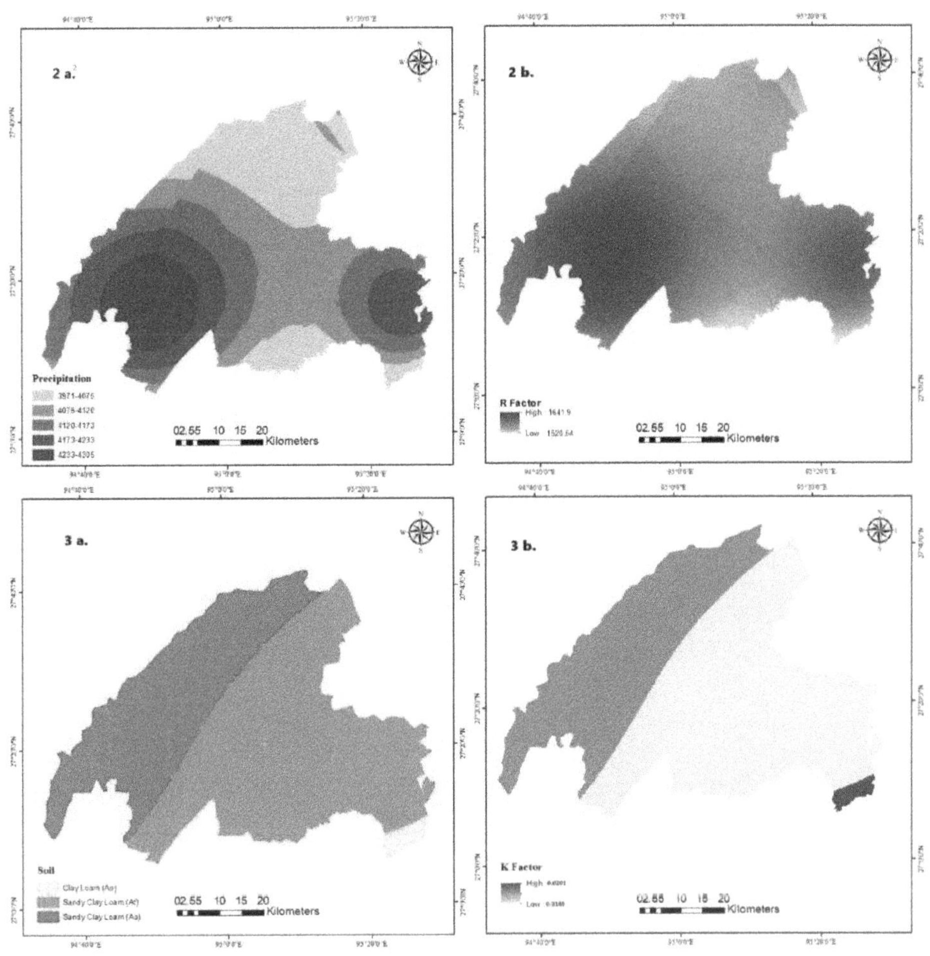

Fig. **2 a:-** Precipitation map; 2 b. R factor map; 3 a. Soil map; 3 b. K factor map

Table 2: LULC types, their areal coverage, and C and P factor value

Type	Shape_Area	Area_Perc	C	P
River bodies	239.513	7.11143	1.000	1.000
Sand deposits	657.014	19.50750	1.000	1.000
Forest	238.741	7.08851	0.004	0.000
Agriculture	967.310	28.72060	0.280	0.000
Plantation	731.886	21.73060	0.080	0.000
Settlement/ Built-up areas	545.542	16.19780	1.000	1.000

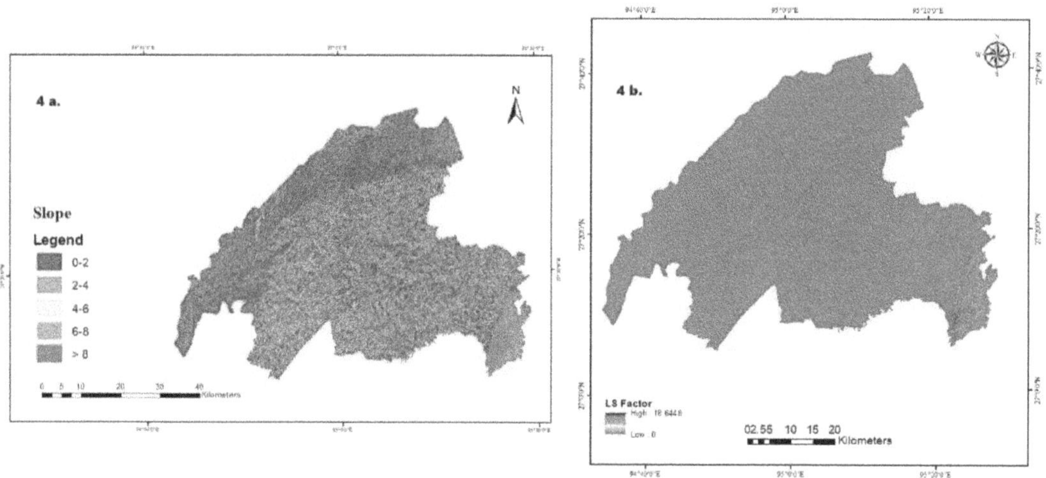

Fig. 4 a: - Slope map; 4 b. LS factor map

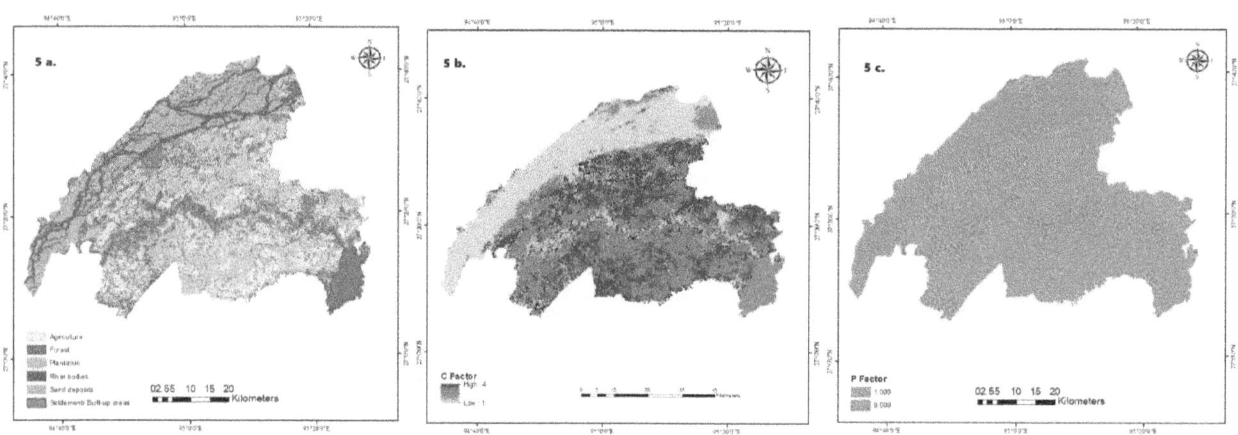

Fig. 5 a:- LULC map; 5 b. C factor map; 5 c. P factor map

Potential Soil Loss in Dibrugarh District:

The soil erosion map (Fig. 6) prepared using eq. 1in ArcGIS 10.8indicated that a vast majority of the area, approximately 91.147%, experiences very slight erosion with a soil loss rate of less than 2 t ha−1 yr−1, encompassing 3006.860 sq. km. This suggests that these areas are relatively stable, with minimal soil degradation. Slight erosion, characterized by soil loss rates between 2 and 10 t ha−1 yr−1, affects 7.638% of the district, covering 251.982 sq. km. Although not critical, these areas may benefit from basic soil conservation practices to prevent further degradation. Moderate erosion, with soil loss rates between 10 and 29 t ha−1 yr−1, was observed in 1.023% of the district (33.738 sq. km). These regions require attention and implementation of soil conservation measures to mitigate erosion. Severe erosion, identified by soil loss rates ranging from 29 to 71 t ha−1 yr−1, affects a smaller portion of the area, making up 0.148% or 4.866 sq. km. These areas are at high risk and require immediate intervention to prevent significant land degradation. Lastly, very severe erosion, with rates exceeding 71 t ha−1 yr−1, was found in only 0.044% of the district, equivalent to 1.466 sq. km (Table 3). These regions face extreme soil erosion and demand urgent and intensive soil conservation efforts to avoid irreversible damage to the land. The study highlights the importance of targeted soil conservation strategies to manage and mitigate soil erosion effectively across the district.

Table 3: Soil severity classes and their areal Coverage

Severity Classes	Area (sq km)	Area (%)
<2 (Very Slight)	3006.860	91.147
2-10 (Slight)	251.982	7.638
10-29 (Moderate)	33.738	1.023
29-71(Severe)	4.866	0.148
>71(Very Severe)	1.466	0.044

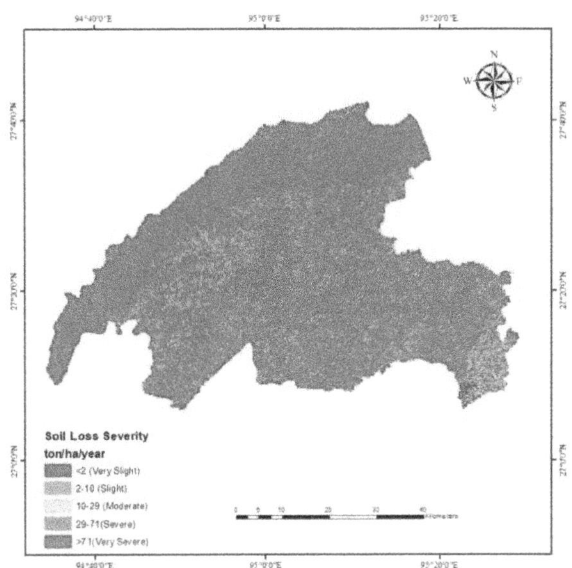

Fig. 6:- Soil loss severity classes of the study area

Conclusion:

In the present study, the RUSLE model was applied in the GIS environment to evaluate soil loss status in the Dibrugarh district of Assam. The results indicate that a majority of the study area (over 91%) experiences a very slight rate of soil erosion, with most areas having erosion rates of less than 2 t ha−1 yr−1. However, small pockets, particularly near riverbanks, exhibited moderate to severe erosion, with rates ranging from 10 to 71 t ha−1 yr−1.The study underscores the importance of utilizing models like RUSLE, integrated with remote sensing and GIS techniques, for effective soil erosion management. These models help identify critical areas requiring intervention and promote sustainable land use and land cover practices.

References:

Ayalew DA, Deumlich D, Šarapatka B, Doktor D. (2020). Quantifying the sensitivity of NDVI-based C factor estimation and potential soil erosion prediction using Spaceborne earth observation data. *Remote Sens*,12:1136.https://doi.org/10.3390/rs12071136.
Benavidez, R.; Jackson, B.; Maxwell, D.; Norton, K. (2018). A review of the (Revised) Universal Soil Loss Equation ((R) USLE): With a view to increasing its global applicability and improving soil loss estimates. *Hydrol. Earth Syst. Sci.*22, 6059–6086.https://doi.org/10.5194/hess-22-6059-2018.

Bora, S.L., Das, J., Bhuyan, K., Hazarika, P.J. (2023). Flood Susceptibility Mapping Using GIS and Multi-criteria Decision Analysis in Dibrugarh District of Assam, North-East India. In: Das, J., Bhattacharya, S.K. (eds) Monitoring and Managing Multi-hazards. *GIScience and Geo-environmental Modelling*. Springer, Cham. https://doi.org/10.1007/978-3-031-15377-8_4.

El Jazouli, A., Barakat, A., Ghafiri, A. et al. (2017). Soil erosion modeled with USLE, GIS, and remote sensing: a case study of Ikkour watershed in Middle Atlas (Morocco). *Geosci. Lett.* 4, 25. https://doi.org/10.1186/s40562-017-0091-6.

Handique, A., Dey, P., & Patnaik, S. K. (2023). Application of Revised Universal Soil Loss Equation (RUSLE) model for the estimation of soil erosion and prioritization of erosion-prone areas in Majuli Island, Assam, India. *Journal of Applied and Natural Science*, 15(4), 1667-1678.http://dx.doi.org/10.31018/jans.v15i4.5176.

Jayasekara M. J. P. T. M,Kadupitiya H. K., Vitharana U. W. A (2018), "Mapping of soil erosion hazard zones of Sri Lanka," *Tropical Agricultural Research*, vol. 29, no. 2, pp. 135–146. https://doi.org/10.4038/tar.v29i2.8284.

Negese, A.; Fekadu, E.; Getnet, H. Potential Soil Loss Estimation and Erosion-Prone Area Prioritization Using RUSLE, GIS, and Remote Sensing in Chereti Watershed, Northeastern Ethiopia. *Air Soil Water Res.* 2021, 14, 1178622120985814.https://doi.org/10.1177/1178622120985814.

Pandey, A., Chowdary, V. M., & Mal, B. C. (2007). Identification of critical erosion prone areas in the small agricultural watershed using USLE, GIS and remote sensing. *Water resources management*, 21, 729-746.https://doi.org/10.1007/s11269-006-9061-z.

Renard KG, Foster GR, Weesies GA, McCool DK, Yoder DC (1996) Predicting soil erosion by water: a guide to conservation planning with the Revised Universal Soil Loss Equation (RUSLE). Agric Handb, 703:25–28.

Renard, K.G.; Foster, G.; Weesies, G.; McCool, D.; Yoder, D. (1997). Predicting Soil Erosion by Water: A Guide to Conservation Planning with the Revised Universal Soil Loss Equation (Rusle); United States Department of Agriculture: Washington, DC, USA, Volume 703.

Sarma, K., & Dutta, P. J. (2021). Soil erosion estimation of Palasbari in northeast India by RUSLE Model.*Bulletin of Pure and Applied Sciences*, 40 (2). http://dx.doi.org/10.5958/2320-3234.2021.00012.3.

Sharpley, A., Williams, J. (1990). EPIC-erosion/productivity impact calculator: 1. model documentation (p. 1768). Washing ton: US Department of Agriculture. https://lib.ugent.be/catalog/rug01:000223279.

USDA-SCS. (1972). 'Hydrology' in SCS national engineering handbook, section 4. Washington DC: US Department of Agriculture.

Wijesundara, N.C., Abeysingha, N.S., Dissanayake, D.M.S.L.B (2018). GIS-based soil loss estimation using RUSLE model: a case of Kirindi Oya river basin, Sri Lanka. *Model. Earth Syst. Environ.* 4, 251–262. https://doi.org/10.1007/s40808-018-0419-z.

Wischmeier, W. & Smith, D., (1978). Predicting rainfall erosion losses—A guide to conservation planning.USDA Agricultural Handbook, No. 537.

Wischmeier, W. H. and Smith, D. D., (1978). Predicting Rainfall Erosion Losses: A Guide to Conservation Planning. Agriculture Handbook, n. 537, Agriculture Research Service, US Department of Agriculture, Washington, DC, USA. 58 pp.

Wischmeier, W., & Smith, D. (1957). Factors affecting sheet and rill erosion. Transactions. American Geophysical Union, 38(6), 889–896.

CHAPTER 3

Existing Status of Solid Waste Generation and its Management System in Itanagar Capital Region (ICR), Arunachal Pradesh

Ligang Aniya and Tage Rupa Sora

Abstract:

Generating a huge quantity of waste is a serious concern in many urban areas. Management of waste particularly solid waste is one of the growing potential problems in most urban regions. Itanagar Capital Region (ICR) is facing a similar problem regarding managing the huge amount of waste generation and its disposal. In the present study, the existing status of solid waste generation and its management system has been analyzed in the capital region of Itanagar using both primary as well as secondary sources of data. The household survey was conducted using a simple random sampling method and a questionnaire was prepared to collect primary data. The entire 20 wards of Itanagar Municipal Corporation (IMC) were surveyed and found that the average per capita waste generation in the surveyed household is 450 gm/day. The study found that Ward no. 9 generates the highest per capita waste among all other wards i.e. 580 g/day. The study revealed that the total amount of waste generated from Domestic, Bio-medical, and Industrial units in the study area is 58,042.07 kg/day (58tons/day).Managing such a huge amount of waste is a serious problem in the study area. The existing waste management system of the region is suffering from various deficiencies. Despite serious attempts, IMC is unable to manage the problem of solid waste efficiently. The region is still witnessing a lot of problems related to the collection, transportation, treatment, and disposal of waste. Unscientific ways of waste disposal through open dumping need to be stopped and proper landfill sites should be selected to dispose of the waste collected. Thus, the present study may help decision-makers understand the present scenario of waste generation and management systems of the study area to adopt appropriate strategies and manage the problem of solid waste sustainably.

Keywords: - Management, Solid Waste, Landfill, Unscientific.

Introduction:

Waste is any material that is disposed of when essentially utilize, or is squandered, impotent, and of no utilization (Gajendra, 2018). These materials are unusable to human beings for a particular purpose (Manohar, 2018). Solid waste is those organic and inorganic waste materials produced by various societal activities (Madhavrao, 2016). It consists of a mass of heterogeneous discarded materials from domestic, commercial, industrial, and agricultural activities (Jeyapriya, 2008). Around 2.1 billion metric tons of Municipal Solid Waste (MSW) is generated annually worldwide (Nichols & Smith, 2019). It is expected that the world generation of MSW will increase to around 3.4 billion metric tons by 2050 (Kaza et al., 2018).With the population projected to grow continuously and increasingly concentrated in urban areas, the rates of waste generation will continue to accelerate, becoming a high-priority concern for both human health and the natural environment. Hence, sustainable and integrated waste management is a major concern in many developing countries.

In the capital Region of Itanagar, the solid waste management system is the concern area of the Itanagar Municipal Corporation (IMC) established under the IMC Act 2007to provide necessities to the people including a clean and green environment. Hence, tackling the problems of solid waste management is one of the areas of its major concern. Presently Itanagar Capital Region has 20 municipal wards, 12 wards located in Itanagar, 6 wards in Naharlagun, and 1 ward each in Nirjuli and Banderdewa respectively. The existing waste management system of the Itanagar Capital Region seems to suffer from various deficiencies. Despite serious attempts, IMC is unable to yield the desired result. The region is still witnessing a lot of problems related to the collection, transportation, treatment, and disposal of waste. Inadequacy in services provided for waste management has made the state rank at rock bottom in the list of the 27 states in the Swachh Survekshan, 2023. The Swachh Survekshan, an annual urban sanitation survey conducted by the Ministry of Housing and Urban Affairs has ranked the state's capital Itanagar431, in the list of 446 cities with more than one lakh population that were judged for their cleanliness performances during the year. Such a scenario has essentially made it significant to understand the existing system of waste management in the study area in a comprehensive manner. The present study is an attempt to understand the status of waste generation and its management system in the Itanagar Capital Region and to suggest effective strategies to improve waste management practices in the area.

Study Area:

The study area, Itanagar Capital Region is the administrative capital city of the state located in the district of Papum Pare. Geographically the area is located between 27°01'58" to 27°11'30" N latitude and 93°29'01" to 93°49'52" E longitude and covers an area of about 213.88 Km².The study area is mostly characterized by highly dissected hills and valleys with rugged topography. Due to the influence of Himalayan topography, the study area experiences tropical to sub-tropical climatic conditions with hot and humid at the lower altitude and extremely cold conditions at the higher altitude. Pachin and Dikrong are the two major rivers drained in the study area. The area receives heavy rainfall from the southwest monsoon.

Figure 1.1 Location of the Study Area

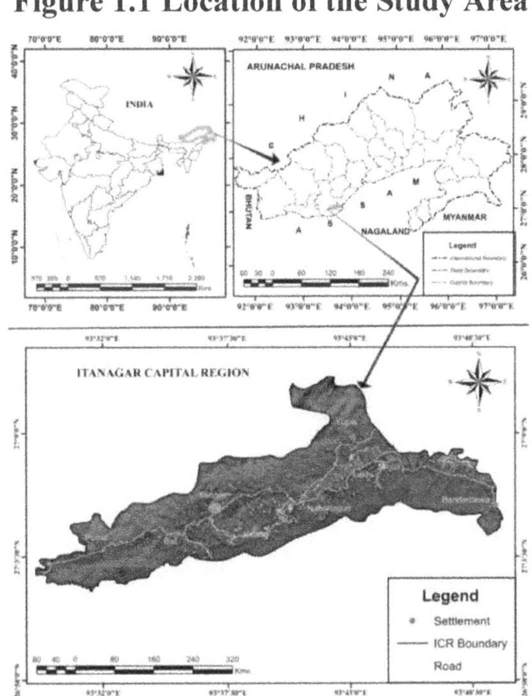

Methodology:

To fulfill the objectives of the study, a questionnaire was prepared and the household survey was conducted for primary data collection. The household survey was carried out for a detailed study of waste management systems in the study area by following a simple random sampling method. A total of 200 household samples were collected, 10 households from each ward. The questionnaire mainly included questions related to the amount of waste generated by households, waste segregation, time and frequency of garbage vehicle services, availability of public bins, environment, and health impact of solid waste etc. To examine the bio-medical waste generated in the study area, a total of 13 Health Care Centers of ICR have been visited and relevant data were collected. Further, data were also collected from reliable secondary sources such as the district statistical handbook, the Census of India report, books, journals, etc. All the collected data were analyzed and presented in tabulation and graphical representation using an MS Excel spreadsheet.

Table 1.1 Ward-wise population of Itanagar Capital Region (Census 2011)

Region	Ward No.	Population as per (2011 census)
Itanagar	1	5441
	2	5256
	3	5263
	4	4506
	5	4809
	6	5061
	7	5072
	8	4958
	9	5136
	10	5102
	11	4724
	12	4895
Naharlagun	13	5289
	14	5994
	15	5660
	16	5803
	17	5821
	18	5870
Nirjuli	19	3686
Banderdewa	20	3426
Total		**101772**

Source: Itanagar Municipal Corporation, 2021

Results and discussion:

The quantity of waste generation in any area is largely determined by its population size, levels of urbanization, and the socio-economic status of the people (Nanda and Berruti, 2021).The study area has witnessed a significant increase in the number of populations in recent decades. The total population of the Itanagar Capital Region in 2001 was 80,536 which has increased to 122,930 in 2011with 62,075 male populations and 60,855 female populations. Among the three circles viz., Itanagar, Naharlagun, and Banderdewa, Itanagar had the highest population (39,173) followed by Naharlagun (35, 211) and Banderdewa (6,152) (Census of India 2001). Since 2001, there has beenan increase in the population in three circles viz. Itanagar (65,301), Naharlagun (49,106) and Banderdewa (8523) in 2011. Even the urban population of the Itanagar Capital Region shows an increasing rate. In 2001 the total urban population was 62,042 which increased to 95,648 in 2011. There has also been an increase in the rural population from 18,494 in 2001 to 27,282 in 2011. With such an increase in the population, the amount of waste generation has also increased. For the quantification of waste generated in the study area, the present study considered mainly three sections i.e. Domestic, Bio-medical, and Industrial waste.

Quantity of domestic waste generation:

The quantity of waste generated from the domestic sector constitutes a significant proportion of the total waste generated in the area. The average per capita waste generation in the surveyed household is shown as 450 gm/day. However, there is variation in per capita waste generation in each ward due to variations in the size of the population (Table 1.2)

Table 1.2Amount of domestic waste generated from surveyed households

Region	Ward No.	No. of Surveyed Household	No. of Population in Surveyed Household	Quantity generation (kg/day)	Average per capita value (gram/capita/day)
Itanagar	1	10	58	30.5	520
	2	10	42	19.8	470
	3	10	52	17.8	340
	4	10	52	23.6	450
	5	10	41	20.2	490
	6	10	40	18.9	470
	7	10	49	22.9	460
	8	10	41	19.6	470
	9	10	49	28.9	580
	10	10	58	20.6	350
	11	10	40	18.8	470
	12	10	44	19.9	450
Naharlagun	13	10	44	22.2	500
	14	10	41	18.3	440
	15	10	45	19.4	430
	16	10	49	25.1	510
	17	10	37	18.2	490
	18	10	56	21.5	380
Nirjuli	19	10	49	17.9	360
Banderdewa	20	10	46	15.9	340
Total		200	933	420.3	`

Source: Field Survey

Table 1.2 shows the amount of waste generated from 200 surveyed households. The waste generated amount was calculated for 933 persons residing in 20 different wards of Itanagar Municipal Corporation who generate around 420.3 kg of waste per day. Ward no. 9 generates the highest per capita waste among all other wards i.e. 580 g/day followed by Ward no.1 and Ward no. 16 i.e. 520 and 510 g/day respectively. Areas included under these wards are Niti Vihar, Mowb-I, Mowb-II, Bank Tinali, Heema Hospital, 0 Point Tinali market (**Ward no. 9**), Chimpu, Forest Colony, Zoo Road, IRBN headquarter, Statistical Colony, Gopur Tinali (**Ward no. 1**) and E-Sector, G-Extension, Power House Colony, Forest Colony, F- Sector, G-Sector (**Ward no. 16**).

Total domestic waste generation:

Total Population of Itanagar Capital Region as per 2011 Census = 1,22,930

Per Capita waste generation rate = 0.45 kg/day (450 gm/day)

Total Domestic Waste Generation = 0.45 x 1,22,930

$$= 55,318.5 \text{ kg/day (55 tons/day)}$$

Quantity of bio-medical waste generation:

Bio-medical waste comprises solid or liquid waste that is generated from various healthcare establishments such as hospitals, nursing homes, clinic dispensaries, veterinary institutions, etc. (Dehal et al. 2022). Waste generated from bio-medical activities is mostly hazardous and toxic and poses a high potential risk for disease transmission (Vasistha, 2018). Therefore, proper disposal of bio-medical waste is very crucial so that it does not mix with other municipal waste. Bio-medical waste generated from the study area is shown in (Table 1.3).

Table 1.3 Quantity of Bio-Medical Waste Generated in Capital Region

Itanagar Capital Region	Name of Health Care Centers (HCCs)	Quantity of Bio-medical Waste Generation(in kg/day)				
		Yellow	Red	White	Blue	Total bio-medical waste generated (kg/day)
Government HCCs	PHC Chimpu	0.3	0.05	0.1	1.1	1.6
	UPHC, Itafort	0.66	0.33	0.1	0.82	1.91
	Regional Ayurveda Research Institution, Itanagar	0.03	Nil	0.11	Nil	0.14

	TRIHMS, Naharlagun	356	85	43	56	540
	UPHC, Rakap	0.4	0.05	0.07	1.1	2
	Dispensary PTC, Banderdewa	0.2	0.03	0.1	0.03	0.4
Private HCCs	RKM Hospital, Itanagar	47	55	Nil	22	121
	Heema Hospital, Itanagar	1.4	0.1	Nil	0.3	1.8
	Ambee lab, Itanagar	0.1	0.04	0.1	0.1	0.3
	Niba Hospital, Naharlagun	1	2	0.02	2	5
	E.B.T. M Hospital Naharlagun	1.37	1.1	2.2	0.8	5.47
	Samaritan Hormin Hospital	2.74	10.96	2.74	27.39	43.83
	Tago Memorial Institute of Health Science and Hospital, Nirjuli	Nil	0.1	0.01	0.01	0.12
Total		**411.2**	**111.6**	**154.76**	**48.45**	**723.57**

Source: Annual Report 2019-2020, State Pollution Control Board (SPCB

As per the survey conducted in the Capital Region, a total of 13 hospitals were covered of which 6 hospitals were Government Health Care Centers and 7 hospitals were Private Health Care centers. Among the government health care centers, Tomo Riba Institute of Health and Medical Science (TRIHMS) generate the highest amount of biomedical waste i.e. 540 kg/day (Table 1.3). Drastic increases in the quantity of biomedical waste have been witnessed amidst the COVID-19 situation. Various private health care centers are also providing medical services in the study area which generates a significant amount of biomedical waste in the area. Ramakrishna Mission Hospital, Itanagar is one such private Health Care Center that generates the highest amount of biomedical waste among all private Health Care Centers i.e. 121 kg/day. The study area generates different types of bio-medical waste among which generation of yellow waste is the maximum i.e. 411.2 kg/ day followed by blue waste i.e. 111.6 kg/day. Red and white waste generates about 154.76 kg/day and 48.45 kg/day respectively. The study area generates total bio-medical waste of about 723.57 kg/day (Arunachal Pradesh State Pollution Control Board, 2020) which demands proper management for its disposal. The absence of such management can cause serious health hazards in the area.

Quantity of industrial waste generation:

For the present study, two industrial units located in the study area were surveyed and their waste generation rate was recorded (Table 1.4). The industrial unit located at Lekhi, Naharlagun manufactures Ferro Alloys. The production of ferroalloys mainly generates waste in the form of slag, dust, and sludge (Zhdanov et al. 2015). The manufacturing industry located at Lekhi generates Silica fumes as a by-product or waste. A considerable amount of around 833 kg/day of waste is generated daily from this industry. Though, reportedly these wastes are recycled for making white bricks. However, if such a huge amount of waste is not managed properly it can cause harmful impacts on human health with its frequent exposure through inhalation, ingestion and skin contact (Ahmad et al. 2023).

Another industry located in the study area is the iron and steel factory located in Banderdewa. This factory generates a huge amount of solid waste such as pretreatment slag, dust, scrap, muck, and debris. As per the information furnished, around 1167 kg/day of waste is generated from this manufacturing unit.

Table 1.4 Quantity of Industrial Waste Generation

Sl. No.	Name of Industries	Location	Manufacturing	Quantity of Waste generated (kg/day)
1.	Shree Salasar Industries	Lekhi, Naharlagun	Ferro Alloys	833
2.	Satyyam Steel and Alloys	Banderdewa	Iron and Steel	1167
Total				**2000**

Source: Field survey

Waste Generation in the Study Area:

The total amounts of waste generated from Domestic, Bio-medical, and Industrial units in the study area are:

Domestic waste = 55,318.5 kg/day

Bio-medical waste = 723.57 kg/day

Industrial waste = 2000 kg/day

Total = **58,042.07kg/day (58 tons/day)**

The study area generates a total amount of 55,318.5 kg of domestic waste per day which includes all biodegradable and non-biodegradable waste generated from domestic households. Bio-medical waste from hospitals, clinics dispensaries, nursing homes, etc. generates a total amount of 723.57 kg/day and industrial units generate a total amount of 2000 kg/day. Altogether, these three sectors in the study area generate a total amount of 58,042 kg of waste per day which constitutes 58 tons of waste generation per day. Such a huge generation of solid waste requires a proper management system to protect the environment as well as to enhance public health.

Management of solid waste in the Itanagar Capital Region:

Management of waste involves proper handling of generated waste through various stages of generation, collection, handling and transfer of waste to processing and treatment to its disposal (Nanda and Berruti, 2021). The way generated wastes are managed by an individual or authority reflects their concern for the environment or human health. In the study area, wastes generated from different sources are managed differently according to the nature of the waste.

Management of domestic waste:

Domestic waste constitutes the highest amount of waste generated in the region. In the study area, domestic wastes both biodegradable and non-biodegradable are managed differently.

Management of Biodegradable Domestic Waste in Surveyed Households

The survey conducted in the study area shows that biodegradable waste generated from surveyed households issued as compost, fodder for animals and collected by municipal garbage vehicles for final disposal (Table 1.5).

Table 1.5 Management of Biodegradable Waste in Surveyed Household

Management of Biodegradable Waste	No. of Household	Percentage
Compost for Kitchen Garden	34	17
Use as Fodder	42	21
Collected by Garbage Vehicle	124	62
Total	**200**	**100**

Source: Field Survey

As per the survey conducted, 34 households which constitute 17% of the total surveyed households, responded that biodegradable wastes generated from their households are used as compost for kitchen gardens while in 42 households, biodegradable wastes are used as animal fodder to feed domesticated livestock such as pigs.

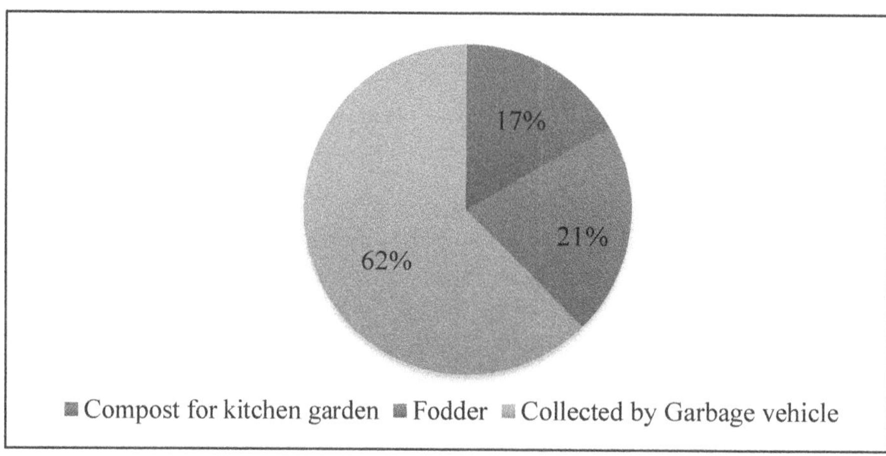

Figure 1.2 Management of Biodegradable Waste

Ward no.20 recorded the highest numbers of respondents revealing that biodegradable waste (food and vegetable waste) generated from their houses is mostly used for animal fodder as most of the people are engaged in commercial livestock rearing. These areas include Dree colony, Banderdewa 5/1, Dolicoto, Forest colony, and lower Dobum (Ward no. 20). The Survey also reported that biodegradable waste generated from hotels and restaurants in these areas is collected by people and used as fodder for their animals. However, responses from 124 households revealed that biodegradable wastes are collected by municipal garbage vehicles for disposal at the dumping site. In most areas of Itanagar and Naharlagun, it was found that biodegradable waste which can be managed by people with proper segregation ended up at dumping sites.

Management of Non- Biodegradable Waste:

The survey conducted in the study area revealed that, in 24 households, non-biodegradable wastes generated from their houses are collected by rag pickers (Table 1.6). Rag pickers in the study area mostly collect non-biodegradable waste such as plastic bottles, cans, metals, etc. for recycling purposes. In most places, people responded that they burn most of the non-biodegradable waste generated from their households. In the total of 46 surveyed households, it was found that non-biodegradable waste such as plastics and other combustible waste is often burned outside their household. Responses recorded from 130 households reveal that all of their non-biodegradable wastes generated are collected by Municipal garbage vehicles.

Table 1.6 Management of Non – Biodegradable Waste in Survey Household

Management of Non – Biodegradable waster	No. of Household	Percentage
Collected by rag pickers	24	12

Burn	46	23
Collected by IMC	130	65
Total	200	100

Source: Field survey

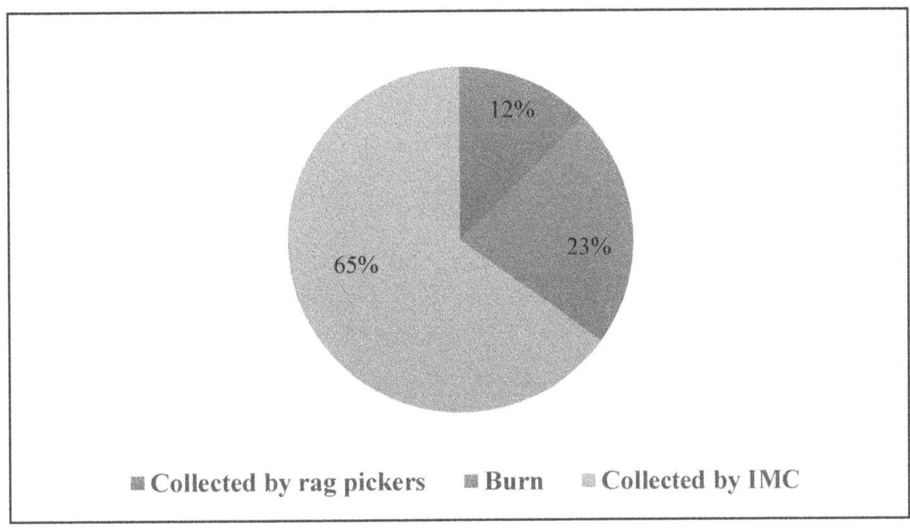

Figure 1.3 Management of Non- biodegradable Waste

Management of Bio-medical waste:

For proper management of Bio-medical waste, it is essential to segregate different components of waste according to their physical, chemical, and biological nature into different colour-coded containers (Kumar et al. 2014). During the survey conducted in 13 Health Care Centers of ICR it was found that in most of the HCC, different colour coding containers such as Yellow, Red, White, Blue, and Black were used for the collection of different bio-medical waste and different treatment facilities are installed for managing these bio-medical wastes. Some of the bio-medical waste treatment facilities installed in various health care centers of the Itanagar Capital Region are shown in (Table1.7).

Table 1.7 Bio-medical Treatment Facilities in Government Health Care Centers (HCCs)

Name of HCCs	Installed Treatment Facilities				Nos.
	Incinerator	Autoclave	Deep Burial	Any Other	
PHC, Chimpu	Nil	2 nos.	1 no.	Needle tip cutter	4
UPHC, Itafort	Nil	2 nos.	1 no.	Needle tip cutter	4
Regional Ayurveda	Nil	Nil	Nil	Needle tip cutter	1

Research Institution, Itanagar				concrete pit	1
TRIHMS	Nil	Nil	1 no.	Needle tip cutter and concrete pit.	35
UPHC, Rakap	Nil	2 nos.	1 no.	Needle tip cutter	4
Dispensary PTC, Banderdewa	Nil	Nil	1 no.	Needle tip cutter and Sharp encapsulation.	1

Source: Annual Report 2019-20, State Pollution Control Board (SPCB)

Table 1.7 shows the total installed biomedical treatment facilities in different government Health Care Centers. The report shows an absence of incinerators in all government Health Care Centers. However, in some hospitals, Autoclaves are used for decontaminating certain biological waste. A total of 6 autoclaves were installed 2 each in the hospital of PHC Chimpu, UPHC Ita Fort, and UPHC Rakap. In most of the hospitals, deep burial was practiced for handling biomedical waste except in the Regional Ayurveda Research Institution Itanagar. Besides these, many needle tip cutters, sharp encapsulation, or concrete pits are used in these hospitals.

Table 1.8 Bio-medical Treatment Facilities in Private Health Care Centres (HCCs)

Name of HCFs	Installed Treatment Facilities				
	Incinerator	Autoclave	Deep Burial	Any Other	Nos.
RKM Hospital	1 no.	2 nos.	1 no.	Needle tip cutter	11
Heema hospital	Nil	2 nos.	Nil	Needle tip cutter,	4
				concrete pit	1
Ambeelab, Itanagar	Nil	Nil	Nil	Needle tip cutter	1
Niba Hospital	Nil	1 no.	2 nos.	Needle tip cutter	4
E.B.T.M Hospital	Nil	2 nos.	2 nos.	Shedder,	2
				Needle tip cutter,	2
				and Concrete pit	1

Samaritan Hormin Hospital	Nil	Nil	Nil	Needle tip cutter	5
Tago Memorial of Health Science and Hospital, Nirjuli	Nil	3 nos.	Nil	Needle tip cutter,	3
				Microwave	1

Source: Annual Report 2019-20, State Pollution Control Board (SPCB)

Among all the private health care centers, installation of the incinerator was found only in Ramakrishna Mission Hospital, Itanagar. The hospital being the highest waste generator among all private Health Care Centers in Itanagar has installed an incinerator for proper handling of bio-medical waste with a capacity of 20 kg/day. A total of 10 Autoclaves were installed in different private hospitals except in Ambee Lab Itanagar and Samaritan Hormin Hospital, Naharlagun. Deep burial was practiced in RKM Hospital, Niba Hospital, and E.B.T.M Hospital and several needle tip cutters, shedders, and concrete pits were used in these hospitals.

Management of Industrial waste:

Two industrial units considered for the present study generate a considerable amount of waste in their process of manufacturing the final products. Wastes generated from these industries are managed differently. The Ferroalloys industry produces Silica fume as a by-product which is recycled for making white bricks. As per the information given, a huge amount of silica fume is collected and stored which is later sent to Guwahati for making white bricks.

Iron and steel industries generate a huge amount of slag, but granulated slag is recycled in making different building materials such as bricks, concrete aggregates, glass-ceramic tiles, wall materials, etc. Scrap metals generated during manufacturing processes have high recycled value hence, they are not just wasted rather reuse for the production of different metal products after melting in the furnace. Therefore, though the two manufacturing industries of the area generate a huge amount of waste, most of them are recycled before ending up in the disposal site.

Problems associated with the waste management system in ICR:

Management of solid waste is one of the most challenging tasks with a significant addition of population every year. In the process of a waste management system, there are challenges at each stage starting with the segregation of waste at the source, collection, transportation and disposal. Management of solid waste in the Itanagar Capital Region is facing similar problems. Despite serious attempts, the region is dealing with several difficulties, some of the problems are.

The problem of source segregation:

Segregation of waste before its collection is the most necessary practice that should be adopted. Waste segregation helps in reducing the amount of waste generation by facilitating recyclable materials. The study area generates various types of waste such as organic, inorganic, recyclable, and non-recyclable. These wastes can be well segregated to manage properly. However, segregation is not practiced by most of the residents in the study area due to which waste generated from the region is collected by Municipal Corporations in a mixed state. Lack of awareness among people is the root cause of non-segregation of waste. As per the data collected through the questionnaire, about 62% of the sampled households do not segregate their wastage at home.

Lack of infrastructure:

The lack of proper infrastructure is one of the major factors affecting the existing waste management system in the capital region. Infrastructure facilities in terms of garbage vehicles, recycling plants, or treatment plants are either limited or there are none in the study area. There is a need to increase the number of garbage vehicles as the existing numbers are not enough to provide service to the entire region.

Recycling waste from unwanted material for resource recovery is very essential in any waste management system. In the study area, some rag pickers collect reusable waste materials such as plastic bottles, cans, metals, etc. for recycling purposes. However, these sections of people could not collect all recyclable materials generated from the region. Due to bulk waste collection, it becomes very difficult for them to sort different waste types before their disposal. Hence, the informal sector participating in the waste management system needs to provide with required economic and institutional support. Resuming the function of the lone existing treatment plant of Chimpu is another concern in the management system. The treatment plant which was established in 2013 has stopped operating since 2014 mainly due to technical problems which has resulted in the disposal of untreated waste in an open ground.

The study area generates a significant amount of domestic waste which mostly constitutes compostable waste. These wastes can be treated by composting, through which they can be recycled in natural form by returning organic matter to the soil. However, the absence of a compost plant or compost pit is another constraint in the study area. Due to the lack of compost plants most biodegradable waste generated from residential kitchens, restaurants, vegetable vendors, etc. are disposed of in the open ground.

Technical and operational constraints:

The feasibility of technology not only depends on financial instability but also technical and operational capability. There is a shortage in the numbers of trained and qualified workers under Itanagar Municipal Corporation who have a predominant responsibility in dealing with the existing waste management system. Most of the workers of IMC are not trained adequately. This has resulted in a lack of data maintenance regarding waste generation, collection, and disposal (Table 1.9).

Table 1.9 Status of Skilled and Unskilled Workers under IMC

Workers	No. of Workers	Working as	No. of Workers
Male	80	Helper	10
Skilled	3	Sweeper	62
Unskilled	77	Lifter	65
Female	77	Driver	20
Skilled	0		
Unskilled	77		
Total	**157**		

Source: Itanagar Municipal Corporation, 2021

Table 1.10 Status of Sanitary Assistants and Drivers Working under IMC

Sub–Division / Office	Nos. of Sanitary Assistant	Nos. of Drivers
Itanagar Sub-Division- I	26	05
Itanagar Sub- Division- II	29	03
Itanagar Sub- Division- III	28	02
Naharlagun Sub-Division- I	33	04
Naharlagun Sub- Division- II	29	05
Office	12	01
Total	**157**	**20**

Source: Itanagar Municipal Corporation, 2021

The above data furnished by IMC reveals that out of 157 workers working under IMC 80 are male workers and 77 are female. Technical deficiency is revealed in the data which shows only 3 skilled male workers. Out of a total 157 workers, 154 are unskilled and need proper formal training. At present, there are only 20 drivers, whereas, the number of sanitation garbage vehicles is 44. Shortfalls of 24 drivers are managed by engaging sanitary staff. Though a proposal for the recruitment of more drivers has already been made by concerned authorities such operational and technical constraints can create loopholes in the overall functioning of a planned system.

The problem of uncontrolled disposal:

Open dumping and burning of waste in open space is the common method adopted for the disposal of waste in the capital region. Location of any dumping ground should be located 200m away from highways (Solid Waste Management Rules, 2016). However, the dumping ground of Itanagar Capital Region is located just 50m away from NH415 which is not in abidance with Waste Management Rules. The practice of such uncontrolled waste disposal gives rise to a substantial health hazard and causes irreparable damage to the environment by polluting land, water, and air. The practice of open dumping is a violation of Solid Waste Management Rules, 2016 which prohibits open dumps and directs municipal authorities to dispose of solid waste in an engineered landfill. Lack of insufficient space for the disposal of waste is another problem faced in the area. The area dedicated to dumping ground is limited and hence needs a bigger space where a proper landfill can be done.

Conclusion:

The present study revealed that the study area generates 450gm of waste per day on average and ward no. 9 generates the highest per capita waste of 580 gm/day. The existing waste management system in the study area is lacking in many aspects. Deficiency in the management system is witnessed bya lack of trained and qualified workers, a lack of infrastructure development in terms of garbage vehicles, recycling plants or treatment plants, and technical and operational constraints. Most vehicles used for waste collection are frail and need to be upgraded along with increasing their numbers. In addition, people in the area lack adequate awareness about waste management policies, including waste segregation at its source. Hence, un segregated waste collection is one of the major problems hindering its management system in the area. Due to technical and operational constraints, the collection of waste and movement of vehicles are not properly monitored by concerned authorities creating loopholes in the entire management system. Non- biodegradable and non-recyclable wastes are the most hazardous waste due to their inability to decompose which makes them last for hundreds of years. Hence, recycling of waste should be focused in the area so that more waste can be recycled before its final disposal. The practice of waste disposal is another problem in the area as collected waste is disposed of unscientifically in an open dumping ground. Therefore, proper landfill sites should be selected to dispose of collected waste at scientific landfill sites and not dumped in open ground.

Referenced:

Ahmad, W., Zubair, M., Ahmed, M., Ahmad, M., Latif, S., Hameed, A., & Iqbal, D. N. (2023). Assessment of potentially toxic metal (loid) s contamination in soil near the industrial landfill and impact on human health: an evaluation of risk. *Environmental Geochemistry and Health*, 45(7), 4353-4369.

Dehal, A., Vaidya, A. N., & Kumar, A. R. (2022). Biomedical waste generation and management during COVID-19 pandemic in India: challenges and possible management strategies. *Environmental Science and Pollution Research*, 1-16.

Gajendra, N (2018). An economic analysis of solid waste management a study of Bengaluru city. Tumkur University, Bengaluru.

Kumar, R., Gupta, A. K., Aggarwal, A. K., & Kumar, A. (2014). A descriptive study on evaluation of bio-medical waste management in a tertiary care public hospital of North India. *Journal of Environmental Health Science and Engineering*, 12, 1-7.

Manohara, B. (2018). Physicochemical and spectroscopic characterization of municipal solid waste composting process, University of Mysore.

Madhavrao, W. P (2016). Material use and recycling comparative study of waste management in Nanded city, SwamiRamanand Teerth Marathwada University, Maharastra.

Jeyapriya, S. P., & Saseetharan, M. K. (2008). Energy recovery from municipal solid waste in an anaerobic reactor. *Journal of Environmental Science and Engineering*, 50(3), 235-238.

Nanda, S., & Berruti, F. (2021). Municipal solid waste management and landfilling technologies: a review. *Environmental chemistry letters*, 19(2), 1433-1456.

Nichols, W., & Smith, N. (2019). Waste generation and recycling indices 2019: Overview and findings. *Verisk Maplecroft, United Kingdom*.

Kaza, S., Yao, L., Bhada-Tata, P., &Van Woerden, F. (2018). *What a waste 2.0: A global snapshot of solid waste management to 2050*. World Bank Publications, p.3.

Vasistha, P., Ganguly, R., & Gupta, A. K. (2018). Biomedical waste generation and management in public sector hospital in Shimla City. In *Environmental Pollution: Select Proceedings of ICWEES-2016*, Springer Singapore, 225-232.

Zhdanov, A. V., Zhuchkov, V. I., Dashevskii, V. Y., & Leont'Ev, L. I. (2015). Problems with waste generation and recycling in the ferroalloys industry. *Metallurgist*, 58, 1064-1070.

CHAPTER 4

Reviving Stilwell Road: A Review on its Prospects and Challenges

Manngam Wangpan, Rani Cheda, Habung Hagio, and Sailajananda Saikia

Abstract

The Stilwell Road also known as Ledo Road connects Assam in India to Yunnan Province in China, passing through northern Myanmar. It was used as a route for Trans – regional movement between Assam and Myanmar till early 19th century. The road was initially used as an alternative route to the Burma and China by the Allied Soldiers, later on it also became a major trade route connecting India to its eastern neighbors. However, the halt in its function since the declaration of the independent nations due to several political and security reasons have crippled the full utilization of the road, which could become the major gateway for trade and other inter-regional prospects.

This paper reviews the prospects and challenges of reviving the Stilwell Road for cross-border trade, and also analyses its importance in the 'Act East Policy'.

Keywords: Stilwell Road, Arunachal Pradesh, Northeast Region, Act East Policy, Myanmar, China.

Introduction:

The Stilwell Road also known as Ledo Road was built during the World War II by an army of 15,000 American soldiers and 35,000 locals under the expert supervision of General Vinegar Joe Stilwell. The road traverses through the distance of 1,736 kms, 57 kms in India, 1,040 kms in Myanmar and 639 kms in China **(Yhome, 2015)**.

"The Stilwell Road Project once termed as an 'Impossible Engineering pipe dream' was not merely an Engineering feat accomplished but a saga of valour, grit and determination. It stands as a testament to the Men responsible and the indomitable human spirit that made it possible." This is the inscription at the Jairampur Cemetery in Changlang district, the largest Cemetery dating back to the

Second World War and at the cemetery lie the remains of hundreds of Men who gave up their lives during the building of this Road. Amongst the dead were Indians including many local Tribals, Chinese, Americans and Burmese.

Starting on December 1, 1942, the construction of the road was completed on May 20, 1945. This Project was undertaken at a time when the Japanese were in possession of most of Burma and were inching forward towards India and Southern China. There were already Plane lifts from the North East India to China over what was then called the 'Hump', the impenetrable Hills and Jungles of the Patkai Range and it was through this Patkai Range that the Road was to be built. Ledo was the last Railhead of the Indian Railways and the Road was proposed to be started from there for the same reason. Therefore, the road was built during World War Two to deliver arms and supplies to the Chinese regime as an alternative to using an air route called The Hump, which involved Allied Forces flying from Ledo in India over the eastern Himalayas to Kunming.

The road passed through some of the most difficult mountainous terrains of the world having 700 bridges over big and small rivers. As most of Myanmar was in Japanese hands it was not possible to acquire information as to the topography, soils, and river behavior before construction started. The information was acquired during the road construction only **(Geraldine 2012; Webster 2005)**.

Gradually, after the war, the geopolitical scenario changed the region, dividing the Stilwell Road to fall into three countries, leaving the road largely inactive compared to its wartime functions and utility. The geostrategic position and historical significance of the road has made many consider it as a major gateway for the south Asian counties to enhance bilateral relationships and trade amongst them. India has also recognized the importance of the link road and few initiatives were taken to rejuvenate it. However, very little implementation and results of such policies have been reflected in redevelopment of the road.

Under Prime Minister Narendra Modi, the Look East Policy evolved into the Act East Policy, emphasizing strong, result-oriented diplomacy to further India's interests in the Eastern region. This shift aimed to replace a fragmented approach with proactive measures for concrete geostrategic and geo-economic outcomes. In Arunachal Pradesh, the policy has sparked optimism among academics, policymakers, and stakeholders, encouraging a new paradigm. Additionally, the Stilwell Road, overlooked during the Cold War, has gained prominence for cross-border trade and regional cooperation.

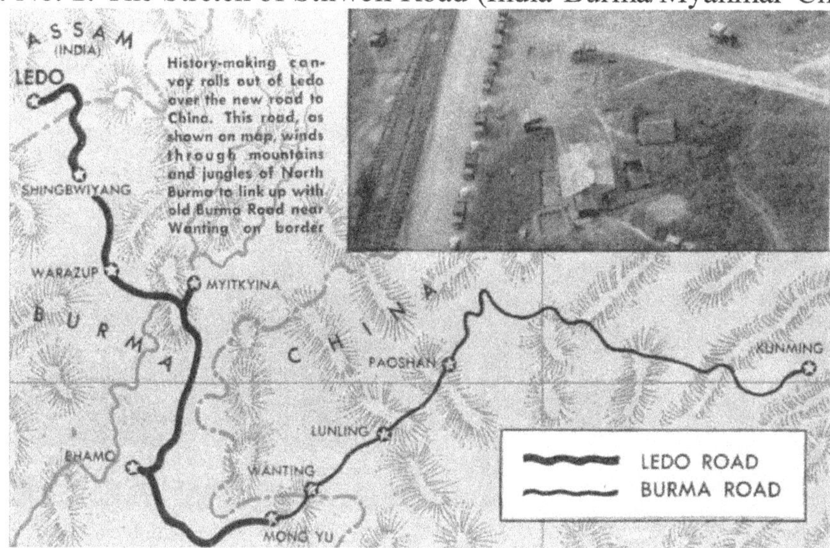

Source: Wayne Whittaker (1945)

Stilwell Road During the War Times:

During the World War II, the China-Burma-India (CBI) Theater was home to many Indians, Americans, British, Africans, Chinese, Burmese, Nepalese, Japanese etc, also including local tribal populations of Nagas, Garos, Chins, Kachins etc. Thus, the whole area was actually a mingling pot of cultures during the World War II. The North East Region played a significant role in the world history. In that theater, the Ledo Road project was not only a road project, it was an important milestone in the history

When Ledo Road was completed, it became one of the most ambitious projects ever done by an army during the war time.The road only became a possibility as it was a desperate situation and the desperate situation needed a desperate solution. The solution was called the Ledo Road only to be renamed later as the Stillwell Road. The road the then was used by the Western Allies to supply arms and war aids to the Chinese to counter the advancing Japanese troops to Burma (Myanmar).The road was also symbolized the cooperation and strong unity between the United States, China, and India. Originally named the 'Ledo Road', as it was constructed under the direct supervision of American General Joseph Warren Stilwell, and was renamed after him in early 1945 at the suggestion of Generalissimo Chaing Kai-shek of China.

Post-War Decline of the Stilwell Road:

After the Second World War, the strategic use and importance of the Stilwell Road diminished considerably. In the course of time, the Stilwell Road had virtually disappeared due to the road lies in the lands of three different nations that are China, Burma and India and due to non-maintenance by the respective nations**(Changlang.nic.in)**.The movement of goods from India and Burma to China was not necessary afterwards, and also the onset of Cold War created tension between Burma and China which reduced the road's utility as it was politically not feasible to use the link route because of political tensions.

Since the end of World War-II, the road has remained inactive, and as a result of subsequent geopolitical events (Partition, Occupation of Tibet and the Indo-China War of '62), mandarins in New Delhi saw little value in it. There is barely any trade activity on this road, besides the barter of goods among people on either side of the Indo-Myanmar border at the Pangsau Pass **(Wangchuk, 2018).**

The geopolitical shifts and change in logistical priorities of the independent nations then led to negligence of the Stilwell Road which was once a significant route of both political and economic aspects. Much of the road has been swallowed up by jungle, barely negotiable on foot, with jungles encroaching the paths which were once perfectly cleared and a standard route for military utility. The decline was quick and so obvious that by the late 20th century, much of the road was considered unfit and unsafe for any mode of transportation. The negligence and under utilization of the road encouraged station of various ethnic insurgents along the India-Myanmar region which also added to the road being deemed dangerous for any communication and transportation through this road **(Bhaumik, 2011)**.

Despite the decline of the Stilwell Road, it remains as a significant symbol of the historic World War and represents its wartime strategic importance.

Present Status of the Stilwell Road:

Since the beginning of the 21st century, the Burmese government focused on the reconstruction of the Ledo Road as an alternative to the existing Lashio-Kunming Burma Road. The border between Assam and Arunachal Pradesh has 14 km of the road section previously which was in deplorable condition, now it is repaired and the construction of international trade route is underway to link Myanmar at Pangsau Pass (Changlang). In India side, the road is being repaired and renovated up to Nampong under this scheme and extension of the renovation work up to Pangsau Pass, Indo-Myanmar border is underway. A Rangoon-based Yazuna Company constructed the section between Myitkina and Tanai (Danai) which was already operational in 2011. The road section from Myitkyina to China border was reconstructed by a Chinese company, from China border to Kunming is a 6-lane highway

Indian government has proposed this road for reopening as International Highway for trade route to link Myanmar (Burma), China and other Southeast Asian countries in its Act East Policy. It has focused on rejuvenating the Stilwell Road to improve connectivity with Southeast Asia and East Asia. The road's revival is expected to boost cross-border trade, enhance regional cooperation, and foster economic development in the northeastern states of India and neighboring regions.

Trade Through Stilwell Road:

The Pangsau Pass stands at the Stilwell Road as the border crossing between India and Myanmar, bearing witness to waves of migrations over the centuries. Although the road remained majorly disused after the war, it was accessed by the locals for basic trade and local movements across the border. While the written record of the locals and their aftermath use of the road is scarce in the literature domain, the enduring cultural and social affinity of the border communities and their shared economic relationships till date stands as a proof of the historical trade across the border and most likely through the Stilwell Road.

Gradually in the 21st century, the trade and cross-border movement became more evident. Because the nearest town in Myanmar is about 60 km away, connected by the old Stilwell Road, which is nearly impassable during the rainy season, the locals of Myanmar visit the Indian side for procuring needful itemsatPangsau Pass. At this Pass, 'Burma Day' was celebrated every Friday which allowed villagers to cross into India and visit Nampong market for essentials. Additionally, Indian citizens could visit Pangsau village on the 10th, 20th, and 30th of each month, known as 'India Days,' with a market featuring Burmese products and local foods like leafy vegetables, sticky rice, and rice noodle soups. The Arunachal Pradesh government, in consultation with the Indian Army, determined these access days **(Rahman, 2016).**

Towards ushering in regional cooperation, the Stilwell or Ledo Road was reopened on 30 December, 2015. One Chinese truck, accompanied by two light motor vehicles, carrying electronic goods, organic tea, coffee, and toys crossed the Pangsau Pass en route to Guwahati to take part in the Assam International Agri-Horti Show **(Pao, 2024).**

Following the 1962 Sino-Indian War, the border routes of Arunachanal Pradesh were mostly closed due to security reasons, including the NampongPangsau Pass were closed which resulted in interruption of cross-border interactions. Gradually in the late 1980's the government of India realized the importance of the eastern trade corridor and focused on India-Myanmar trade prospects. The governments of India and Myanmar signed an agreement in 2003 to promote border trade through designated points, including the Pangsau Pass. This agreement aimed to revitalize the historical trade route and strengthen economic ties between the two countries. The Common Border Trade Agreement of 1994 and a gradual improvement of the bilateral relationship began taking shape. In 1995 India and Myanmar even conducted a joint military operation against ethnic guerrilla groups **(Myint, 2011)**.

The 'Look East Policy', which focused on eastern neighbours and Asian markets and expansion of Indian trade relations towards Southeast Asia pushed many factors of border trade development along the Nampong-Pangsau Pass. The governments of India and Myanmar signed an agreement in 2003 to promote border trade through designated points, including the Pangsau Pass. This agreement aimed to revitalize the historical trade route and strengthen economic ties between the two countries **(Naidu, 2010).**In January 2009, the Pangsau Pass was officially reopened for border trade after decades of closure. This event marked a significant step towards restoring the historical trade route and enhancing cross-border economic activities **(Bhatia, 2015).**And, in 2019, India announced several development projects to enhance connectivity and trade infrastructure along the border with Myanmar, including improvements to the Stilwell Road and the Pangsau Pass. These projects aimed to boost economic activities and support local communities on both sides of the border **(MEA, 2019)**.

One of the measures that was expected to provide thrust to the 'Act East' policy was the reopening of the historic Stilwell Road that had linked North East India to China through northern Myanmar during World War II. Despite considerable efforts, little progress was made, and the hope of reopening the Stilwell Road is still a staggering path **(Saikia, 2023)**.

In the most recent hopeful event, Governor KT Parnaik of Arunachal Pradesh visited Nampong town and advocated for the resumption of border trade activities at Pangsau Pass in Changlang district. Trade at Pangsau Pass was halted following the Covid-19 outbreak in 2020 **(Arunachal Times, 2023).**

Prospects of Trade through Stilwell Road:

The very ambitious 'Act East Policy' of India, has called for a proactive step towards developing not only bilateral relationships but also stressing on exploring the economic opportunities with its eastern neighbors. This has raised the hopes in developing the eastern corridor as well as the border trade aspects, especially by opening the major routes in the border regions such as Stilwell Road.

The Stilwell Road, running from Assam in India to Myanmar and further on to China, could act as a growth driver for the entire region. India's 'Act East' policy should factor in this road while planning for new developments in this region. This road has the potential to break the landlocked status of Northeast Region (NER). Goods from NER normally pass through the narrow Siliguri Corridor to

Kolkata covering about 1600 km and then transshipped again through the Strait of Malacca to Southeast Asia and China. The present route takes nearly seven days for the landing of cargo, whereas the same consignment through Stilwell Road can land in Myanmar and China in less two days **(Pattnaik, 2024).**

If the Stilwell Road goes operational, the NER will have direct access to markets in China, Myanmar and various Southeast Asian countries. As stated earlier, the one can reach Kunming in two days using this road. It will take two and a half days to reach Yangon, the capital city of Myanmar, while Bangkok will take four days and Singapore in five-six days. Compared to sea routes, this land route is expected to be shorter and more cost-effective for international trade. Policymakers advocating for the reopening of this road believe it will attract significant investment to the Northeast Region, providing a pathway out of the current economic malaise. **(Wangchuk, 2018).**

The connectivity through Stilwell Road offered can majorly contribute to the goals of 'Act East Policy'. It can involve Myanmar as the buffer and gateway as the same time to engage with the ASEAN nations. This connectivity can also encourage greater people-to-people communication not only through trade but through tourism and other socio-cultural activities as most of the border population on the either side shares close cultural affinity. This would help in promoting bilateral relation and connecting the countries.

The Stilwell Road presents a substantial opportunity for Northeast India, especially the states of Assam and Arunachal Pradesh, to transform their economies by opening up trade and commerce with China and ASEAN countries. Reviving border trade at Pangsau Pass, along the Myanmar border, will reduce the time, cost, and distance involved in trade. This initiative may also encourage mainstream Indian industries to invest in production hubs in Northeast India, manufacturing goods for export to China and Southeast Asia. Consequently, Northeast India has the potential to become a regional hub where neighboring countries can obtain Indian automobile components, pharmaceuticals, fruits, vegetables, textiles, and cotton yarn. Conversely, Indian traders will gain access to electronic gadgets, blankets, consumer durables, teak, gold, and semi-precious stones from the other side. Also, it will be in better interest of India to develop the infrastructure and its portion of the Stilwell road, as accrued commercial interests are likely to outweigh the pros of its non-construction **(Puyam, 2015).**

Accelerating economic growth in the Northeast hinges on the reopening of the Stilwell Road, enabling people to tap into trading opportunities with Asian countries, including China. Northeast India holds a strategic geographic advantage for boosting border trade with Southeast Asia and China. Cities like Kunming, Bangkok, and others in Myanmar and China are closer to this region than to Delhi, Mumbai, or Bangalore. The key to leveraging this advantage is the long-awaited restoration of the Stilwell Road at Ledo, which connects Assam to Kunming and other Southeast Asian metros. Reopening this route could significantly increase trade with these countries and potentially transform the area into a Special Economic Zone (SEZ) **(Sinha, 2010).**

Restoring trans-border communities through border and inter-country trade is essential, and industrialization in the region should also be emphasized. Accelerating economic growth in the Northeast hinges on reopening the Stilwell Road, enabling people to explore trading opportunities with Asian countries, including China. Although many Northeastern states are economically underdeveloped, Assam stands out due to its substantial natural resources, including vast deposits of crude oil and natural gas, as well as its significant tea production. Additionally, Assam produces high-quality Eri, Muga, and mulberry silk, all of which have great demand in the global market **(Phukan, 2015).**

Underscoring the importance of re-opening historic Stilwell Road, Deputy Chief Minister Chowna Mein on Sunday said that it would serve as catalyst for cross border trade, deepen age-old cultural linkage and help promote spiritual tourism **(Behera, 2020).**

The Northeast India is a resource rich and less explored region. Its potentials like oil, natural gas, coal, silk, tea, horticulture, floriculture, biodiversity tourism, tribal and ethnic artifacts trade promise a bright economic progress if the development in forms of infrastructure, proper governance and border friendly policies are implemented. Therefore, the re-operation of the Stilwell Road may create new avenues for trade and commerce, additionally building people-to-people contact in the region across border. The opening of the road will assuredly give access to the commercially potent ASEAN markets under the Act East policy.

Challenges of Cross-Border Trade through Stilwell Road:

Act East Policy is expected to lead the NER into the new era of development through connectivity, communication and trade. The strive to overcome the state of being landlocked and ensure progress of the region through physical connectivity is ridden by both prospects and challenges.

Despite many opportunities, several obstacles have hindered the development of Northeast India both in the past and in recent times. Words like 'alienation', 'exploitation,' and 'insecurity' are used throughout the region due to various are underlying issues such as insurgency. This has kept the area in a constant state of unrest, lacking the political and economic stability essential for meaningful progress, thereby negating the benefits of the limited economic development that has occurred **(Sinha, 2010).**

The Stilwell Road, historically significant and strategically located, poses several risks as a trade route, particularly when considering its potential reopening for trade between India, Myanmar, and China.

1. Security Concerns: The region of Arunachal Pradesh through which the Stilwell Road passes is infamous for insurgent activities. This poses risk for operating smooth trade and other economic activities along the road and across the border through this road. Additionally, its proximity to the infamous 'Golden Triangle' also threatens drug trafficking and smuggling along the road if the cross-border trade is carried out without standard and strict measures.

2. Political Tension: The proximity of the route can pose threat to geopolitical tensions such as an easy access of China to Arunachal Pradesh, the state which China claims. The ongoing internal political instability of Myanmar can also affect India through Stilwell Road as influx of Myanmar nationals can easily enter India through the route. Moreover, local trade and trading activities along the route may get disturbed due to the geo-proximity of the route.

The route's proximity to the India-China border, particularly in Arunachal Pradesh, a region claimed by both countries, can escalate geopolitical tensions. Trade through this route might be influenced by the broader strategic and diplomatic relations between India and China.

3. Infrastructure Challenges: The maintenance and logistics management of the road maybe difficult as the route is largely located in the isolated regions (India and Myanmar), and the geographical terrain of the route can also pose obstacles in timely maintenance of the road. Moreover, as the Stilwell Road runs through three different countries, the logistics management and transnational communication along the route may be difficult to operate due to underlying political and security reasons.

4. Economic Viability: The reconstruction and reutilization of the Stilwell Road to meet modern trade requirements can require financial investment and major government focus and interest. Also, the proper utilization of the route is not assured. The success of the trade route depends on the demand for goods and the economic interdependence of the regions it connects. Insufficient market access or demand can render the route economically unfeasible.

5. Environmental Concerns: As the Stilwell Road cuts through major biodiversity hotspot, the reconstruction would hamper and disturb the natural environment and many habitats of the rare-endemic species. Deforestation is also a concern if the route is to be developed for modern trade activities.

Addressing these risks requires a comprehensive approach involving security measures, diplomatic negotiations, infrastructure development, and environmental management.

Taking into account the numerous challenges or risks involved in reopening of the Stilwell Road, it becomes imperative to first resolve the issues of conflict between India, China and Myanmar. Trans-border communities can be restored through border trade and inter-country trade and emphasis should be also laid on industrialization in the region.

Conclusion:

Stilwell Road is one of the prime transnational roads in the Indian subcontinent. The re-utilization of this route for trade can boost the Indian border trade aspects towards the eastern neighboring countries making it a major corridor for economic transition and trading and economic hotspot. For this, the government of India, the Border States, especially Arunachal Pradesh must adopt proactive role and work rigorously to provide not only infrastructural support but also political and regional stability.

The participation of the locals and the holistic support from the tri-countries (India-Myanmar-China) would accelerate development of economic spheres along the route, communication and rebinding of culture and above all extending transnational ties. This would not only impact the local socio-economic setting but improve bi-lateral goals of the connecting countries despite all odds.

References:

Yhome, K. (2015). The Burma Roads: India's search for connectivity through Myanmar. *Asian Survey*, *Vol. 55*(No.6), 1217–1240. https://www.jstor.org/stable/26364333

Myint-U, T. (2011). *Where China meets India: Burma and the new crossroads of Asia*. Farrar, Straus and Giroux.

Naidu, G. V. C. (2010). India and Southeast Asia. *International Studies*, *47*(2-4), 285-304.

Bhatia, R. (2015). *India--Myanmar Relations: Changing Contours*. Routlcdgc India.

Geraldine, H. S. (2012). "Highway to Freedom": African Americans in World War II China, the Gillem Board, the Ledo Road and U.S. Racial Integration, (ed. W. R. Allen, R. T. Teranishi and M. Bonous-Hammarth), Advances in Education in Diverse Communities: Research, Policy and Praxis, Vol. 7, Emerald Group Pub. Ltd., pp. 225-234.

Webster, D. (2005). The Burma Road: The Epic Story of the China-Burma-India Theater in World War". New York: Farrar, Straus and Giroux

Stilwell Road (Ledo Road) | Changlang District, Government of Arunachal Pradesh | India. (n.d.). https://changlang.nic.in/stilwell-road-ledo-road/

Wangchuk, R. N. (2018, March 1). *Constructed by the Americans during WW-II, this road could transform the northeast*. The Better India. https://thebetterindia.com/132920/constructed-americans-ww-ii-road-transform-northeast/

Subir Bhaumik, "India not to reopen key WWII road", BBC, August 11, 2009, http://news.bbc.co.uk/2/hi/south_ asia/8194622.stm accessed on July 23, 2024

Zulfiqur Rahman, M. (2017, August 3). *The Abandoned Route Through India, Myanmar and China Should be Restored*. The Irrawaddy. Retrieved July 25, 2024, from https://www.irrawaddy.com/opinion/guest-column/abandoned-route-india-myanmar-china-restored.html

Pao, Panging.M.. (2024, February 18). *author*. https://arunachaltimes.in/index.php/2024/02/18/stilwell-road-and-the-hump-operations/

Ministry of External Affairs (2019, December 19) *India-Myanmar - Bilateral brief*https://www.mea.gov.in/Portal/ForeignRelation/Myanmar22Nov.pdf

Saikia, J. (2023, February 18). *Opinion | Stilwell Road holds the key to India's 'Act East' policy*. News18. https://www.news18.com/news/opinion/opinion-stilwell-road-holds-the-key-to-indias-act-east-policy-7114549.html

Arunachal Times. (2023, December 31). *GoAP has recommended resumption of border trade at Pangsau Pass: Guv*https://arunachaltimes.in/index.php/2023/12/31/goap-has-recommended-resumption-of-border-trade-at-pangsau-pass-guv/

Pattnaik, K.J. (2017, October 16). *Stilwell Road: A Game changer for Arunachal Pradesh?* The Arunachal Times. Retrieved July 25, 2024, from https://arunachaltimes.in/index.php/2017/10/16/stilwell-road-a-game-changer-for-arunachal-pradesh/

Puyam, G. & CAPS. (2015). OPENING STILWELL ROAD: OPPORTUNITIES AND CHALLENGES. In *CAPS INFOCUS*. https://capsindia.org/wp-content/uploads/2021/10/CAPS_Infocus_GP.pdf

Phukan, K. P. (2018, March 9). *Reviving Stilwell Road: Opportunities for Assam*. Retrieved July 25, 2024, from https://www.linkedin.com/pulse/reviving-stilwell-road-opportunities-assam-c-eng-fipe-mie-miie

Behera, P. K. (2020, February 17). *Reopening Stilwell Road to be catalyst for border trade: DyCM | Arunachal Observer*. Arunachal Observer. https://arunachalobserver.org/2020/02/17/reopening-stilwell-road-catalyst-border-trade-dycm/

Sinha, T. (2010). Reviving the Stilwell Road: challenges and opportunities for India. In *IPCS ISSUE BRIEF* (No. 143). Retrieved July 25, 2024, from https://www.files.ethz.ch/isn/114410/IB143-SEARP-Tuli.pdf

CHAPTER 

Impact of Oil Palm Plantation on Traditional Livelihood of East Siang District, Arunachal Pradesh: A Critical Review

Habung Hagio, Manngam Wangpan, and Sailajananda Saikia

Abstract

The United Nation's Sustainable Development Goals clearly underscores the need of synchronising the inter-relationship between economic growth, environmental sustainability and social welfare. In South East Asian countries, the people has immensely benefited from switching to Oil Palm plantation in terms of economic return. Nevertheless, studies clearly indicate that the plantation activities have severely damaged the area both environmentally and socially.

Arunachal Pradesh, the eastern-most state of India, foray into Oil Palm plantation way back in 2012, and East Siang was one of the first districts wherein it was introduced. East Siang district is mainly inhabited by Adi tribe who largely rely on shifting cultivation, settled cultivation (kitchen garden and valley based agriculture) and adjacent forest for their livelihood. Review of literature suggests that introduction of plantation agriculture in general, and Oil Palm plantation in particular, has reoriented the pattern of livelihood from subsistence-based agriculture to monoculture.

In this paper, an attempt shall be made to critically examine the impacts of oil palm plantation on the traditional livelihood of the Adi community of East Siang district from multi-dimensional perspectives. The discussions would be entirely based on secondary data mainly research articles.

Keywords: Oil Palm, East Siang, Traditional Livelihood, Sustainability

Introduction:

Oil Palm (Elaeis Guineensis) is a tropical forest palm native to west and central Africa. The native habitat of oil palm is tropical rainforest with 1780-2280 mm annual rainfall and a temperature range of 24-30∘ C; seedlings do not grow below 15°C (New CROP 1996). The palm thrives in disturbed forest and near rivers; it does not grow well under closed canopies (Corley and Thinker 2003). Oil Palm is tolerant of a wide range of soil types, as long as it is well watered (New CROP 1996).

It is suggested that the oil palm was introduced in Asia sometimes between the 14th and 17th centuries by the European colonizers (Poku 2002). Today, Indonesia and Malaysia are the largest Oil Palm producers of the world and constitute about 90% of the palm oil production.

Oil palm is comparatively a new crop in India. Government of India (GoI) has been making efforts to increase the area of production of oil palm and its production of palm oil to reduce the import dependence of palm oil. Various schemes since 1991-92 has been introduced to increase the production and its area, the most recent being the National Mission on Edible Oils-Oil Palm (NEMO-OP) 2021. The United Nation's Sustainable Development Goals clearly underscores the need of synchronising the inter-relationship between economic growth, environmental sustainability and social welfare. In South East Asian countries, the people has immensely benefited from switching to Oil Palm plantation in terms of economic return. But for places where the majority communities largely depend for their welfare on traditional subsistence-based livelihoods, the economic benefits last only for a few years after transition, while socio-ecological capital, in which the communities had depended and invested most, deteriorated (Santika.T et al.,2019).

Arunachal Pradesh, the eastern-most state of India, foray into Oil Palm plantation way back in 2012, and East Siang was one of the first district wherein it was introduced. East Siang district is mainly inhabited by Adi tribe who largelyrelyon shifting cultivation, settled cultivation (kitchen garden and valley based agriculture) and adjacent forest for their livelihood (Sarangi.S.K.). Traditional livelihoods as defined by Mohapatra are the livelihoods of the indigenous people living in the region. They have developed highly specific livelihood strategies and livings, most adapted to the conditions of their traditional territories as they were reliant on their access to lands, territories, and resources available in their neighbourhood.The Introduction of oil palm could have its implication on the symbiotic relationship between the Adi community and its traditional livelihood.

Objectives-

In this paper, an attempt shall be made to critically examine the impacts of oil palm plantation on the traditional livelihood of the Adi community of East Siang district by conducting a comparative study on oil palm plantation in South East Asia.

Materials and Methodology-

This section provides detailed methodologies of our study and is organised as follows. The first sub-section presents an overview of the study area and primary livelihoods of the study area. The second sub-section presents the data of oil palm and the third sub-section describes the methods used in the study.

> **Study area and district primary livelihoods**

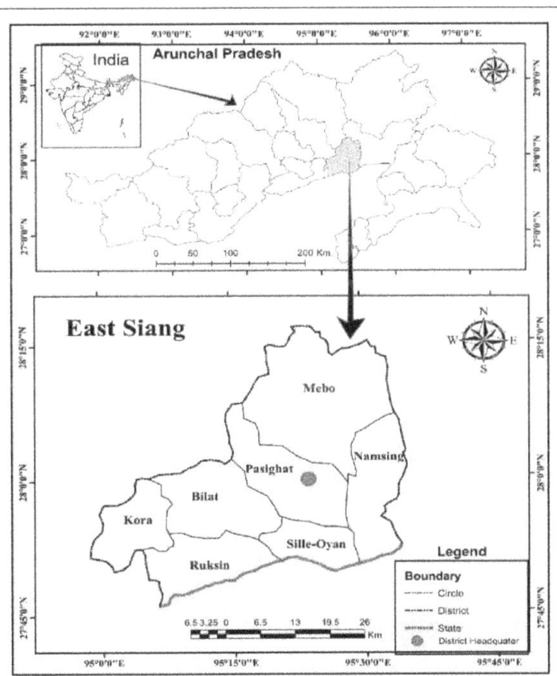

Map- Map showing East Siang District, Arunachal Pradesh

East Siang District is located in the central part of the Arunachal Pradesh and it mainly in habited by the Adi tribes. The district is located approximately in between 27° 43′ to 29°20′ North latitudes and 94°42′ to 95°35′ East longitudes and has an area of 3,603 sq km (60% of land area is cultivable land). The district is mainly inhabited by Adi community of Arunachal Pradesh and agriculture is the main occupation of the people of the district (60% of population is depended on Agriculture for livelihood) and they are largely depended on traditional subsistence based shifting cultivation, adjacent forest and kitchen gardens for livelihood. The main crops grown by the people of the district are paddy, maize, millet and oilseeds. Besides agriculture, the Adi community of the district is also depended on the forest for hunting and gathering which along with the agriculture forms the traditional mode of livelihood and further these activities also play a significant role in the socio-cultural aspect of the Adi community. The festivals that Adi community celebrates such as Mopun, aran or Pombi, Ettor, Lune Solung or Taku-Binnyal and LuttorSolung are interrelated with the subsistence based shifting cultivation practiced by them. Further, Hunting and Fishing stand in the same relation to the domestication of animals as gathering of wild fruits and roots stands to agriculture (S.Roy, 1997).Over the last decade there has been a drastic shift in pattern of agriculture in district, farmers has shifted from shifting cultivation to settled cultivation in many part of the district (Census of India, 2011).

> **Data**

- **Present status of oil palm in East Siang District-**

Various cash-crops has been promoted in Arunachal Pradesh by the government over the period of time, for eg. Cardamom, Jatropha, Rubber, kiwi etc. and oil palm is one of the most recent cash crop promoted by various government schemes. East Siang entered into the plantation of oil palm in 2014 with PatanjaliAyurved Ltd. (earlier Ruchi Soya) setting up a nursery (Mongaby-India,2022). As of April 2023, East siang reportedly has over 1600 hectares of standing oil palm cultivation (Govt. of Arunachal Pradesh) and as per Techno-Economic Feasibility Report (2913-14), the district has a potential area of 24,000 hectare (Undivided East Siang) for oil palm plantation.

Table: Potential Area for Oil Palm in Arunachal Pradesh

	District	Approx. Potential Area (Ha.)
1.	Lohit (undivided)	25,000
2.	Changlang	10,000
3.	Tirap	3,500
4.	Lower Dibang Valley	30,000
5.	East Siang (undivided)	24,000
6.	West Siang (undivided)	12,000
7.	Lower Subansiri	8,000
8.	Papum Pare & East Kameng	19,000
	TOTAL	1,31,500

Source: Techno-Economic Feasibility Report (2013-14

Table- Area under oil palm plantation in East Siang District (2015-23)

Year	2015-16	2016-17	2017-18	2018-19	2019-20	2020-21	2021-22	2022-23
Area (Ha.)	200	450	757	991	1059	1559	1584	1636

Source: Agriculture Department, Government of Arunachal Pradesh

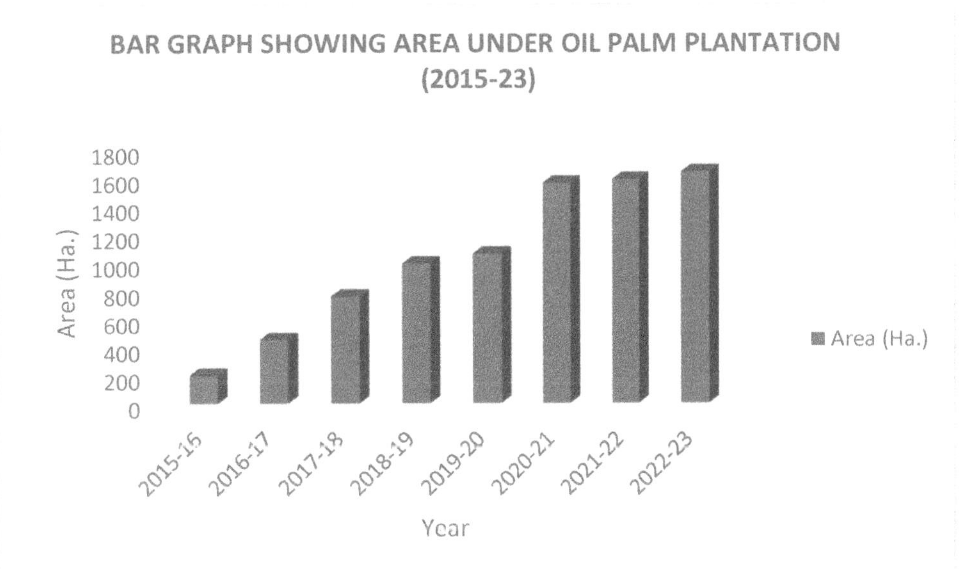

Graph: Area under oil palm plantation in East Siang district.

The introduction of oil palm plantation in the district has been facilitated by various government policies in order to increase the domestic production and decrease the dependence on import. The proposed schemes have advocated the introduction of Oil Palm in fallow and wasteland area of the district (NEDFi final report, 2020). According to Wasteland Atlas of India-2015-16, wasteland in Arunachal Pradesh includes land use such as land with dense and open scrub, shifting cultivation-current and abandoned jhum, degraded pastures/grazing land, degraded forest (scrub domain/agriculture), barren rocky/stony waste and snow-covered area.

Table- Wasteland area of East Siang District 2015-16

Wasteland	Land with Dense scrub	Land with Open scrub	Shifting-Cultivation Current Jhum	Shifting-Cultivation Abandoned Jhum	Degraded Forest	Barren Rocky	Snow Covered

| Area (in sq. km) | 5.15 | 7.69 | 17.45 | 64.43 | | 3.78 | 0.12 |

Source- Wasteland Atlas of India 2015-16.

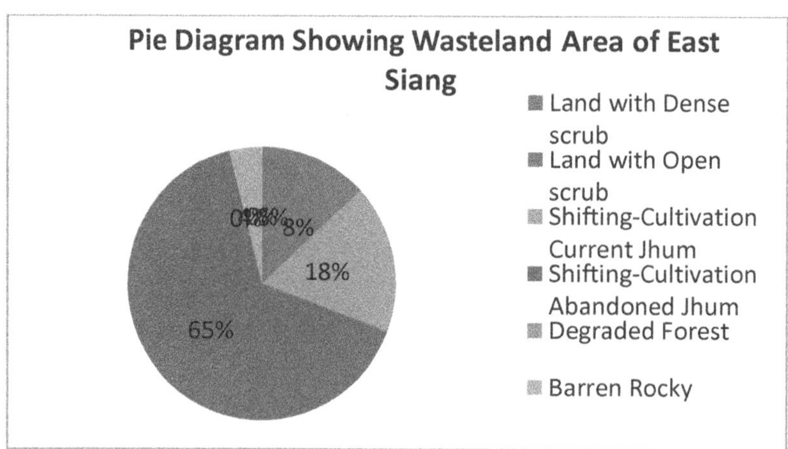

Graph- Pie diagram showing wasteland area of East Siang District, Arunachal Pradesh

From the above given data it is clear that the area under shifting cultivation (both current and abandoned) constitute the largest area which is considered as a wasteland. Therefore it can be can be said that the oil palm plantation proposed by the government will be replacing the area under shifting cultivation in the major part of the district.

- **Impact of oil palm plantation on traditional livelihood in South East Asia**

It is suggested that the oil palm was introduced in Asia sometimes between the 14th and 17th centuries by the European colonisers (Poku 2002). Today, Indonesia and Malaysia are the largest Oil Palm producers of the world and constitute about 90% of the palm oil produced and hence has been playing an important role in the economy of their farmers in particular and the countries in general. The people of South East Asia had traditionally been engaged in paddy cultivation and fishing but they have ceased to exist in many part of the region where oil palm plantation has flourished ever since its introduction. The farmers of the region has transitioned from traditional livelihood activities to oil palm based livelihood primarily due to perceived higher income and perceived ease of managing oil palm plantation (NorwanaDayang.A.A.B, et al 2011).

The livelihood transition to oil palm monoculture was associated with a marked increase in economic benefits for villages with polyculture plantation as the primary sector, especially after 9–11 years of transition, the period when oil palm plantations start to be productive (Koh and Wilcove, 2007). Adequate experience in plantation management, and knowledge of and familiarity with the market economy, are key factors for why the economic benefit from oil palm monoculture was optimal and long lasting among polyculture plantation smallholders. The living conditions in communities improved markedly after transitioning to oil palm monoculture, it has been seen that continuous increase in proportions of household with electricity and improvement in sanitation and cooking fuel up to 9–11 years of transition. Further it was seen that the infrastructure, such as healthcare facilities and schools improved after decade of transition(Santika.T, et al. (2019).

Despite significant gains in economic wealth, the socio-ecological negative implications associated with transition to oil palm were also high, mainly from exacerbated water pollution and decreased community cohesion, i.e. increased influx of agriculture wage labourers from outside the villages as indicated by increased ethnic diversity and reduced voluntary community cleaning and maintenance (gotongroyong). While the local communities could weakly depend on rivers or lakes for drinking water, water pollution could have a detrimental affect on the poorest communities within these villages. Water pollution degrades aquatic ecosystems, and many depend on water bodies as sources of protein, regardless of their major livelihood (Food and Agriculture Organization (FAO, 2011).

On the other hand, for villages that used to depend on traditional subsistence-based livelihoods (farming, foraging and fishing), a move towards oil palm monoculture appeared to be a serious challenge. This can be related to two things. First, these local communities are shaped from a fundamentally different life system than those based on cash crop agriculture. The dependency on forest and natural resources are the main characteristics of villages with traditional subsistence-based livelihoods, thus ecosystem deterioration through increasing water and air pollution and floods from the oil palm industry could have a negative impact on their existence (Mainusch, 2010). Many of these communities also have strong cultural ties with their ancestral livelihoods (Pretty and Ward, 2001), which could make them reluctant to adopt oil palm monoculture. Thus, despite investments and credit opportunities pour into these new oil palmareas at the beginning of oil palm development increasing the economic welfare of the villages overall after transitioning to the oil palm sector relative to the counterfactual, the local communities are unlikely to take advantage of the opportunities and do not benefit from such services. In addition, an influx of agricultural wage laborers from outside the village to fill plantation labour quota could overwhelm the existing facilities that had already been lacking, as reflected by the reduced provision of electricity compared to the counterfactual, and slowing down in the improvement of access to clean sanitation and drinking water after 9–11 years of oil palm plantation development. A growing influx of agricultural labourers could further lead to inequitable competition and displacement of local communities and their traditional culture. Thus, for these subsistence based communities, exacerbation of poverty can be caused not only by isolation from the modern market economy, but also from contact with it (Sunderlin et al., 2005).

> **Methodology**

In this paper study of impact of oil palm plantation on traditional livelihood shall be attempted primarily based on secondary data collected from both published and unpublished sources. The study shall critically review the impact of oil palm plantation in traditional livelihood of farmers based from South East Asia and conduct a comparative study with reference to East Siang district of Arunachal Pradesh.

Results and Discussions-

The Adi community of East Siang district of has since time immemorial been practicing the traditional subsistence based shifting cultivation and it has been their primary livelihood for the same length of time. This mode of agriculture has not only been their main source of food and income but also has huge impact on their culture. Further hunting, fishing and gathering of wild fruits and roots are also facilitated by the very same forest which provides land for shifting cultivation (S.Roy, 1997).

The introduction of oil palm in East Siang district has been facilitated by various government policies. Today the district has about 1600 hectare of its land under oil palm plantation and is estimated to have about 24,000 hectare of land area as potential area. The government has advocated for the introduction of oil palm in the waste land area of the district. As per the Waste Land Atlas (2105-16) Shifting cultivation-current and abandoned jhum is regarded as the predominant waste land area of the district.

As per the review of literature of oil palm and its impact on traditional livelihood of farmers in South-East Asia suggests that the shifting from traditional subsistence based shifting cultivation to monoculture based oil palm plantation has significant economic gain for those having market exposure, while the socio-ecological welfare deteriorated drastically for both the farmers having exposure to market and those who did not (Santika.T et al., 2019).

Adicommunity of East Siang district is predominantly dependant on traditional subsistence based shifting cultivation and hunting and gathering for their livelihood. The introduction of oil palm is been advocated by various government policies to be done on the fellow land the waste land of the district, which according to the 'Waste Land Atlas of India 2015-16' is predominantly composed of the area under shifting cultivation in the district. Thus the introduction of oil palm will have a huge impact on the current mode of sustenance based livelihood and socio-cultural significance associated with it.

It can further be said that the based on the experiences of South East Asia, farmers transitioning from traditional agriculture to oil palm plantation could have gain in economic welfare for those having access to market which is very unlikely because there is no mill to process the Fresh Fruit Bunches (FFB) in the state and further the socio-ecological condition of the district could deteriorate.

Policy Implications-

Oil Palm in East Siang in particular and Arunachal Pradesh in general has been introduced by various government schemes such as National Mission on Edible Oil- Oil Palm (NMEO-OP), with an objective to enhance the edible oilseeds production and oil palm availability in the country by harnessing Oil Palm area expansion, increasing crude palm oil production and to reduce import burden on edible oils. While striving to achieve this goals, the traditional values and culture of farmers has been neglected in the process. The traditional value of shifting cultivation has been completely disregarded while declaring the area under such practice as wasteland land in the wasteland atlas of India. Further policies should also focus on the socio-ecological welfare while trying to achieve the economic aspect of the policy. So the policies that will succeed the present schemes needs to be more people centric and should include the traditional knowledge and values of the farmers at the grassroots level.

References-

Roy.S. 1997. Aspects of PadamMinyong culture, Directorate of Research, Govt. of Arunachal Pradesh, Itanagar.
District Census Handbook East Siang, 2011.Directorate of Census operations, Arunachal Pradesh.
DayangNorwana, A.A.B.,et al.2011 The local impacts of oil palm expansion in Malaysia: An assessment based on a case study in sabah state. Working paper 78. CIFOR, Bogor, Indonesia.
T. Santika, et al. 2019.Changing landscapes, livelihoods and village welfare in the context of oil palm development, Elsevier Ltd.
NEDFi, 2020. Developmental Action Plan for Promoting Oil Palm in the North Eastern Region of India, North Eastern Council, MoDoNER.

CHAPTER **6**

Disparity in Socio-Economic Status: A Comparative Study between the Scheduled Tribe Students from Tawang, Papum Pare and Tirap Districts of Arunachal Pradesh, India

Dipak Sharma, Naitik Kumar Biswas, and Sailajananda Saikia

Abstract

The present study compares the level of socio-economic status (SES) among the Scheduled Tribe (ST) students from Tawang, Papum Pare, and Tirap districts of Arunachal Pradesh with the help of Z-Score statistics and weighted-average methods considering ten parameters as explanatory variables from five different domains (Education, Demographic Characteristics, Geography, Economic Condition, and Social Overhead Capitals). The study was confined to post-graduate students enrolled in the academic session 2019-20 at three higher educational institutions in Arunachal Pradesh- Rajiv Gandhi University (RGU), North Eastern Regional Institute of Science and Technology (NERIST), and National Institute of Technology (NIT). The results showed wide gap in composite Z-score values ranging from -0.20 to 0.27 (Tawang = -0.20; Papum Pare = 0.04; and Tirap = 0.27), respectively. Thus, the findings revealed significant SES disparity between the students from Tawang, Papum Pare, and Tirap, respectively.

Key Words: Arunachal Pradesh; Scheduled Tribe; Students; Socio-Economic Status.

Introduction

In social sciences, socio-economic status (SES) is one of the most widely studied construct (**Bradley & Corwyn, 2002**). SES encompasses two aspects- social status and economic status, and is made up of diverse variables (**Hassan & Akbar, 2020**). And since SES consists not only one but multiple dimensions (**Cutler et al., 2008**), such as social position, prestige, power and economic well-being (**Hoff et al., 2002; Oakes & Rossi, 2003; Conger, 2010**), and hence, SES is regarded as a multidimensional concept (**Gupta et al., 2014**).

Review of literature suggests that there are two issues with the concept of SES. First issue pertains to the conceptual meaning of SES. In other words, there is not a single widely accepted definition of socio-economic status (SES) among investigators (**Kahl & Davis, 1955; Sirin, 2005**). As a result, numerous attempts have been made by eminent researchers and social scientists to put forth a concrete definition of SES. Consequently, a variety of definitions of SES have come into light, for instance, as individual's position within a hierarchical social structure (**Singh et al., 2017**);"one's access to financial, social, cultural, and human capital resources" (**Cowan et al., 2012**); a measure of one's combined social and economic status (**House, 2002; Galobardes et al., 2006**). According to **Hauser and Warren (1997)** and **Muller and Parcel (1981)**, SES not only refers to one's access to economic and social resources but also the social positioning, privileges, and prestige that one derive accessing these resources (**Lerner et al., 2015**).In the view of **Dutton and Levine (p. 30, 1989)**,SES is a "composite measure that typically incorporates economic status, measured by income; social status, measured by education, and work status, measured by occupation" (**Alder et al., 1994**).And recently, SES has been defined as "a broad concept that refers to the placement of persons, families, households and census tracts or other aggregates with respect to the capacity to create or consumer goods that are valued in our society"(**Miech & Hauser, 2001; Shavers, 2007**).

The second issue associated with SES is with regards to measurement of SES. In other words, there is no standard method or measure of SES, and hence, several methods or scales have been proposed since past to measure SES (**Bradley & Corwyn, 2002**). In sociology, SES is regarded as a latent construct and its assessment is done by using a composite measure which incorporates three parameters namely education, income, and occupation (**Baker, 2014**). It is pertinent to note that most of the measures of SES use composite scales, and involve variables from social and economic domains (**Singh et al., 2017**).

Although there is no consensus about the meaning and measurement of SES, yet the need of investigating individual orfamily SES is crucial for two reasons. First, SES is associated with various aspects of an individual's well-being right from to birth and throughout the life course (**Bradley, 2016**). Second is because of the fact that ample research findings clearly demonstrated that SES is positively associated with a wide range of outcomes including health status (**Singh et al., 2017**), health outcomes (**Gupta et al., 2014**), cognitive and socio-emotional outcomes in children (**Bradley & Corwyn, 2002**), school attendance and years of schooling (**Haverman & Wolf 1995, Brooks-Gunn & Duncan, 1997**), academic achievement (**Sirin, 2005**), school achievement (**Hassan & Akbar, 2020**), and so on so forth.

Post World War II, low SES students became a focal point of public policy (**Walpole, 2003**). Review of literature clearly shows that a plethora of work on SES has already been done so far. Nevertheless, students from low SES have not received adequate attention from policy makers, mainly because of the paucity of group identity and political mobilization (**Karen, 1991**). In addition, research works related to students' SES particularly from North-East India in general and Arunachal Pradesh in particular is still scarce in the research domain. In this backdrop, the present study was undertaken during Covid-19 Pandemic with a view to fill the research gap by providing evidence from one of the North Eastern States of India- Arunachal Pradesh.

Objective

The study was undertaken with the following objectives:

1) To determine the level of socio-economic status (SES) of the study populations.
2) To examine whether there is any gradient (disparity) in the level of SES among the study populations.

Research Question

This study aimed to seek answers of the following questions:

1) What is the level of socio-economic status of the study populations?
2) Does the level of socio-economic status of the study populations vary?

Study Area and Population

The present study encompasses three districts of Arunachal Pradesh namely Tawang, Papum Pare, and Tirap. The location of study areas are highlighted in **Figure 1**. Arunachal Pradesh is the easternmost state of India located in the Eastern Himalayas region between 26°30'N and 29°28'N latitudes and 91°25'E and 97°24'E longitudes. It has the largest geographical area (83,743 Sq.km) among all the eight North-East States of India (officially North-Eastern Region). The countries and Indian states which share their border with Arunachal Pradesh are Bhutan to the west, China to the north, Myanmar to the east, Nagaland to the south-east, and Assam to the south. As of January 2021, the state has been delineated into twenty-five administrative districts.

Tawang, with a total geographical area of 2172 sq. km is located between 27° 22' (E) to 27° 45' (E) longitude and 90° 45' (N) to 92° 15' (N) latitude in the western-most corner of the state. The district is predominantly inhabited by the Monpa Tribe (Census 2011).

Papum Pare, also known as the "capital district of Arunachal Pradesh", with a geographical expanse of 3462 Sq.km is the most populated district with Nyishi Tribe forming the majority (Census

2011). It lies in the Lesser Himalayan Zone between 930 12' E to 940 13' E Longitudes and 260 56' N to 270 35' N Latitudes.

Tirap is situated in the southern part of Arunachal Pradesh between 26° 38' and 27° 47' North latitudes and 96° 16' and 95° 40' East longitudes. It has a geographical expanse of 2362 sq. km (approx). Although the district is inhabited by three ethnic groups namely the Nocte, the Wancho and the Tutsa, the Nocte Tribe is the major one in terms of population.

The study areas were purposively selected based on the level of illiteracy or literacy as per Census 2011. For instance, Arunachal Pradesh was first divided into three different belts namely Eastern Belt, Western Belt and Central Belt keeping in view the district's administrative boundaries (**Figure 2**). As per the Census 2011, in the Western Belt and Eastern Belt, the lowest literacy rate was recorded in Tawang and Tirap districts, respectively (**Table 1**). On the contrary, the Papum Pare in the Central Belt recorded the highest literacy rate in the Central Belt as well as across the state. Since the three districts namely Tawang, Papum Pare, and Tirap were unique with respect to literacy rate in their respective belts and hence, these districts were purposely selected as study areas.

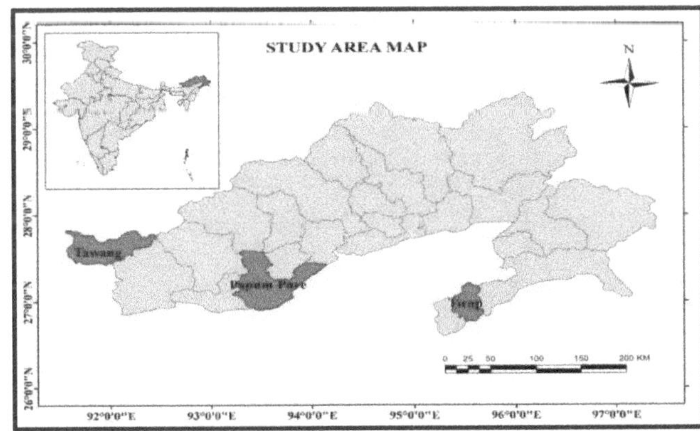

Figure 1: Location Map of the Study Areas	Figure 2: Regional-Division of Arunachal Pradesh

Table 1: Districts by Regional-Belt and Literacy Rate

Regional-Belt	Districts (Census 2011)	Literacy Rate (Census 2011)	Ranking of Districts in terms of Literacy Rate (Census 2011)
Central-Belt	Papum Pare	79.95%	1st
	Lower Subansiri	74.35%	2nd
	East Siang	72.54%	3rd
	Lower Dibang Valley	69.13%	4th

	West Siang	66.46%	5th
	Dibang Valley	64.10%	6th
	Upper Subansiri	63.80%	7th
	Upper Siang	59.99%	8th
	Kurung Kumey	48.75%	9th
Western-Belt	West Kameng	67.07%	1st
	East Kameng	60.02%	2nd
	Tawang	59.00%	3rd
Eastern- Belt	Lohit	68.18%	1st
	Changlang	59.80%	2nd
	Anjaw	56.46%	3rd
	Tirap	52.19%	4th

The target populations in the present study is restricted to only the Arunachal Pradesh Scheduled Tribe (APST) students from Tawang, Papum Pare, and Tirap particularly those that have had enrolled in various post-graduate courses at three higher educational institutions within the state (Arunachal Pradesh) - Rajiv Gandhi University (RGU), North Eastern Regional Institute of Science and Technology (NERIST), and National Institute of Technology (NIT) in the academic session 2019-20.

Materials and Methods

Data Source

First of all, the student data for the academic session 2019-20 was gathered physically by visiting the educational institutions- RGU, NERIST and NIT in the month of October, 2020. This data comprised of student's information such as student's name, domicile state, course pursuing, date and year of enrollment, sex (male/female), telephone/contact number, Gmail address, etc,. This data obtained from the educational institutions, however, did not comprise the students' domicile district's name.

Firstly, all the students of a given educational institution were segregated into two groups- namely APST students and Non-APST Students based on the students' domicile state's name as outlined in the data received from the educational institutions. The list of Non-APST students was kept aside while the list of APST students was taken into consideration for further processing. Afterwards, using the APST student's contact number which was provided by the educational institutions, telephonic interview was undertaken with the main objective to obtain the APST students' domicile district's name. All the APST students enrolled in a given educational institution were then categorized into different groups based on their domicile district's names. Note that the APST students were segregated based on their domicile district's name mainly to frame out the actual population size of the target group under study. The same methodology was followed for the students enrolled in other remaining educational institutions. In total, 1426 students were enrolled in the academic session 2019-20 (RGU- 1107 enrolled students, NERIST- 272 enrolled students, and NIT- 47 enrolled students), of which total Non-APST students and APST students accounted for 466 and 960, respectively. Whereas, about 106 APST students were identified as target populations for the study comprising 16 APST students from Tawang, 68 APST students Papum Pare, and 22 APST students from Tirap, respectively (**Table 2**).

Table 2: Target Population by Their Institutions and Domicile District

(2019-20 Academic Session)

Institutions	R.G.U	N.I.T	N.E.R.I.S.T	Total
Total Enrolled Student	1107	47	272	1426
Total Non-APST Student	279	38	149	466
Total APST Student	828	9	123	960
Total APST Student From Tawang	**16**	**0**	**0**	**16**
Total APST Student From Papum Pare	**49**	**3**	**16**	**68**
Total APST Student From Tirap	**21**	**0**	**1**	**22**
Total APST Student From East Siang	84	1	7	92
Total APST Student From West Siang	54	1	13	68
Total APST Student From Siang	22	1	2	25
Total APST Student From Lower Siang	34	1	7	42
Total APST Student From Upper Siang	30	0	3	33
Total APST Student From West Kameng	27	1	4	32
Total APST Student From East Kameng	39	0	3	42
Total APST Student From Kurung Kumey	34	0	4	38

Total APST Student From Kra Dadi	36	0	4	40
Total APST Student From Shi Yomi	9	1	1	11
Total APST Student From Longding	15	0	0	15
Total APST Student From Dibang Valley	7	0	0	7
Total APST Student From Lower Dibang Valley	35	0	3	38
Total APST Student From Lower Subansiri	123	0	33	156
Total APST Student From Upper Subansiri	41	0	4	45
Total APST Student From Leparada	20	0	7	27
Total APST Student From Anjaw	4	0	1	5
Total APST Student From Namsai	18	0	1	19
Total APST Student From Lohit	12	0	1	13
Total APST Student From Kamle	17	0	2	19
Total APST Student From Pakke-Kessang	5	0	1	6
Total APST Student From Changlang	25	0	1	26

Source: Primary data (telephonic interview, 2020).

Since the study was conducted during Covid-19 Pandemic in the month of December, 2020, the Google-Form was used as online questionnaire and the questionnaire-link was sent via Gmail address to the target populations- the APST students from Tawang, Papum Pare and Tirap for obtaining data entailed for determining the level of Socio-Economic Status (SES). Hence, it is pertinent to note that this study is not based on sample but rather based on the entire target population.

Statistical Method for Measuring the Level of Socio-Economic Status (SES)

Taking cognizance of the literature, the Z-Score statistical method has been used for measuring the level of SES. The formula for deriving Z-scores is presented below:

$$Z = (X - \bar{X})/ SD_x$$

Where,

Z = Z score

X = Raw Score

$$\bar{x} = \text{Mean}$$

$$SD_x = \text{Standard Deviation}$$

Explanatory Variables used for Assessing the Level of Socio-Economic Status (SES)

Family income, parental education, and parental occupational status are the three core measures of students' socio-economic status. Nevertheless, these three measures can also be extended by adding other relevant measures (**Cowan et al., 2012**). Keeping this in view, in total, ten variables from five different domains have been taken into consideration as key explanatory variables for determining the level of socio-economic status of the students. The five domains and ten variables includes education (literacy rates and parental years of schooling), demographic characteristics (family type and sex composition of the second generation), geography (place of residence- rural and urban), economic condition (family monthly income, main source of family income, and family expenditure on health per head per annum), and social overhead capitals (type of the main road which connects the native place to nearest town/city and availability of formal educational institutions within the radius of 1 km from native home).

Levels of Measurement and Weights applied to SES Explanatory Variables

It is worth mentioning that the explanatory variables are measured on three different scales- arithmetic mean, percentage, and weighted-average. The weighted-average technique is applied because some of the explanatory socio-economic variables have been assigned weights. And the prime motive behind weighting to variables in the present study is very straightforward, that is, variable-weighting helps in achieving a more precise estimation of the causal effects of independent variables (for instance literacy rates, parental education, family type, sex, family monthly income, the main source of family income, etc) on the dependent variable (level of socio-economic status) (**Solon et al., 2015**). In the present study, the weighting and weighted-average method have been applied to socio-economic variables including family type (*Nuclear- 0. 60% and Joint- 0. 40%*), place of residence (*Rural- 0.30% and Urban- 0.70%*), family monthly income (*Below 10,000 INR- 0.03%, 10,000 - 25,000 INR- 0.07%, 25,000 - 50,000 INR- 0.15%, 50,000 - 75,000 INR- 0.20%, 75,000 - 1 Lakh INR- 0.25%, Above 1 Lakh INR- 0.30%*), the main source of family income (*Government Service- 0.50%, Business- 0.25%, Agriculture- 0.10%, Others- 0.15%*), family expenditure on health care per head per annum (*Below 10,000 INR- 0.03%, 10,000 - 25,000 INR- 0.07%, 25,000 - 50,000 INR- 0.15%, 50,000 - 75,000 INR- 0.20%, 75,000 - 1 Lakh INR- 0.25%, Above 1 Lakh INR- 0.30%*),and type of the main road which connects the native place to the nearest town (*Rural Road- 0.10%, District Road- 0.15%, Expressway- 0.20%, State*

Highway- 0.25%, National Highway- 0.30%). Nevertheless, it is to be noted that the variables have been assigned weights not based on the standardized weighting-scheme but based on rationality and intuitionistically. For instance, the rural population and urban population are assigned different weights, that is, a higher weight to the urban population (70%) than the rural population (30%). It is because of the fact that urban areas are usually equipped with sound social overhead capitals such as all-weather roads, health, educational facilities, power, transportations, and communication, etc. than rural areas. Keeping this in view, if the proportion of population A is more concentrated in urban areas than population B, signifies that population A has a relative advantage in terms of place of residence than population B. Hence, urban population has been given higher weights than the rural population.

Results

The descriptive statistics of all the independent variables for the Z-score statistics are presented in Table 3.

Table 3: Descriptive Statistics of SES Variables- All Study Populations

Sl. No.	Variables	Tawang (N- 14)				Papum Pare (N- 66)				Tirap (N- 22)			
		X1	X2	$\bar{X}$/%	SD	X1	X2	$\bar{X}$/%	SD	X1	X2	$\bar{X}$/%	SD
1) Education													
1	Literacy Rate												
	First Generation (%)	0	1	61	-	0	1	58	-	0	1	82	-
	Second Generation (%)	0	1	100	-	0	1	99	-	0	1	98	-
2	Parental Education (Years of Schooling)												
	Father (Mean)	0	17.3	8	6.83	0	22.3	7	7.02	0	18.3	10	5.24
	Mother (Mean)	0	14.3	2	4.50	0	17.3	4	5.24	0	19.3	7	6.42
2) Demographic Characteristics													
3	Family Type												
	Nuclear (%)	0	1	86	-	0	1	55	-	0	1	95	-
	Joint (%)	0	1	14	-	0	1	45	-	0	1	5	-
4	Sex Composition (Second Generation)												
	Males (%)	0	1	43	-	0	1	50	-	0	1	41	-
	Females (%)	0	1	57	-	0	1	50	-	0	1	59	-
3) Geography													
5	Place of Residence												
	Rural (%)	0	1	86	-	0	1	79	-	0	1	86	-
	Urban (%)	0	1	14	-	0	1	21	-	0	1	14	-
4) Economic Condition													
6	Family Monthly Income												

		X_1	X_2	$\bar{X}$	SD	X_1	X_2	$\bar{X}$	SD	X_1	X_2	$\bar{X}$	SD
	Below 10,000 (%)	0	1	7	-	0	1	15	-	0	1	14	-
	10,000 - 25,000 (%)	0	1	14	-	0	1	15	-	0	1	23	-
	25,000 - 50,000 (%)	0	1	29	-	0	1	27	-	0	1	23	-
	50,000 - 75,000 (%)	0	1	21	-	0	1	21	-	0	1	23	-
	75,000 - 1 Lakh (%)	0	1	7	-	0	1	9	-	0	1	5	-
	Above 1 Lakh (%)	0	1	21	-	0	1	12	-	0	1	14	-
7	Main Source of Family Income												
	Government Service (%)	0	1	50	-	0	1	36	-	0	1	77	-
	Business (%)	0	1	0	-	0	1	9	-	0	1	5	-
	Agriculture (%)	0	1	21	-	0	1	27	-	0	1	9	-
	Others (%)	0	1	29	-	0	1	27	-	0	1	9	-
8	Family Expenditure on Health Care Per Head Per Annum												
	Nil (%)	0	1	0	-	0	1	3	-	0	1	5	-
	Below 10,000 (%)	0	1	36	-	0	1	26	-	0	1	45	-
	10,000 - 25,000 (%)	0	1	29	-	0	1	33	-	0	1	32	-
	25,000 - 50,000 (%)	0	1	21	-	0	1	15	-	0	1	9	-
	50,000 - 75,000 (%)	0	1	0	-	0	1	8	-	0	1	5	-
	75,000 - 1 Lakh (%)	0	1	14	-	0	1	6	-	0	1	0	-
	Above 1 Lakh (%)	0	1	0	-	0	1	9	-	0	1	5	-
5) Social Overhead Capitals													
9	Type of Main Road Which Connects Native Place To Nearest Town/City												
	Rural Road (%)	0	1	57	-	0	1	42	-	0	1	64	-
	District Road (%)	0	1	7	-	0	1	23	-	0	1	32	-
	Expressway (%)	0	1	0	-	0	1	2	-	0	1	0	-
	State Highway (%)	0	1	14	-	0	1	14	-	0	1	0	-
	National Highway (%)	0	1	21	-	0	1	20	-	0	1	5	-
10	Formal Educational Institutions (Schools, Colleges, and University) Within 1 Km Radius from Native Home												
	Primary (Mean Count)	0	4	1	0.97	0	6	2	1.30	1	6	2	1.47
	Secondary (Mean Count)	0	2	1	0.84	0	6	1	1.17	0	4	1	1.19
	Higher Secondary (Mean Count)	0	2	1	0.76	0	6	1	1.15	0	1	0	0.29
	Colleges (Mean Count)	0	1	0	0.36	0	6	1	1.31	0	1	0	0.21
	University (Mean Count)	0	6	0	1.6	0	6	0	1.06	0	0	0	0.00

Source: Primary data, 2021.

Note:

1) X_1, X_2, $\bar{X}$, and SD denotes minimum value, maximum value, mean, and standard deviation.

2) The mean and percentage values are rounded-off so as to minimize the cell size.

Since weights have been applied to some variables, a new table has been prepared to show all the socio-economic variables with their assigned weights and measurements in terms of percentage, mean, weighted-averages, and Z-scores for each of the study populations (Table 4).

Table 4: Variable-Weights and Z-Scores: Tawang, Papum Pare and Tirap

Sl. No.	Variables	Weights	Tawang (N- 14)		Papum Pare (N- 66)		Tirap (N- 22)	
			$\bar{X}$/%/WA	Z-Score	$\bar{X}$/%/WA	Z-Score	$\bar{X}$/%/WA	Z-Score
1) Education								
1	Literacy Rate							
	First Generation (%)	-	61	-0.46	58	-0.69	82	1.15
	Second Generation (%)	-	100	1.00	99	0.00	98	-1.00
2	Parental Education (Years of Schooling)							
	Father (Mean)	-	8	-0.22	7	-0.87	10	1.09
	Mother (Mean)	-	2	-0.93	4	-0.13	7	1.06
	Composite Z-Score			**-0.15**		**-0.42**		**0.57**
2) Demographic Characteristics								
3	Family Type							
	Nuclear (%)	60%	53	-0.32	51	-0.8	59	1.12
	Joint (%)	40%						
4	Sex Composition (Second Generation)							
	Males (%)	-	43	-0.35	50	1.13	41	-0.78
	Females (%)	-	57	0.35	50	-1.13	59	0.78
	Composite Z-Score			**-0.10**		**-0.26**		**0.37**
3) Geography								
5	Place of Residence							
	Rural (%)	30%	36	-0.47	38	0.94	36	-0.47
	Urban (%)	70%						
	Composite Z-Score			**-0.47**		**0.94**		**-0.47**
4) Economic Condition								
6	Family Monthly Income							
	Below 10,000 (%)	3%	29	0.00	29	0.00	34	1.73
	10,000 - 25,000 (%)	7%						
	25,000 - 50,000 (%)	15%						
	50,000 - 75,000 (%)	20%						
	75,000 - 1 Lakh (%)	25%						
	Above 1 Lakh (%)	30%						
7	Main Source of Family Income							
	Government Service (%)	50%	31	-0.30	27	-0.82	42	1.12
	Business (%)	25%						
	Agriculture (%)	10%						
	Others (%)	15%						
8	Family Expenditure on Health Care Per Head Per Annum							
	Nil (%)	0%	38	-1.00	39	0.00	40	1.00

No	Variable	WA						
	Below 10,000 (%)	3%						
	10,000 - 25,000 (%)	7%						
	25,000 - 50,000 (%)	15%						
	50,000 - 75,000 (%)	20%						
	75,000 - 1 Lakh (%)	25%						
	Above 1 Lakh (%)	30%						
	Composite Z-Score			-0.43		-0.27		1.28
5) Social Overhead Capitals								
9	Type of Main Road Which Connects Native Place To Nearest Town/City							
	Rural Road (%)	10%						
	District Road (%)	15%						
	Expressway (%)	20%	17	0.38	18	0.76	13	-1.13
	State Highway (%)	25%						
	National Highway (%)	30%						
10	Formal Educational Institutions (Schools, Colleges, and University) Within 1 Km Radius from Native Home							
	Primary (Mean Count)	-	1	-1.15	2	0.58	2	0.58
	Secondary (Mean Count)	-	1	0.00	1	0.00	1	0.00
	Higher Secondary (Mean Count)	-	1	0.58	1	0.58	0	-1.15
	Colleges (Mean Count)	-	0	-0.58	1	1.15	0	-0.58
	University (Mean Count)	-	0	0.00	0	0.00	0	0.00
	Composite Z-Score			-0.12		0.51		-0.38
	Overall Composite Z-Score			-0.20		0.04		0.27

Source: Primary data, 2021.

Note: WA denotes weighted-average; the mean and standard deviation of Z-Score values are equal to zero (0) and one (1).

Figure 3: Composite Z-Scores of the Study Populations in Five Domains

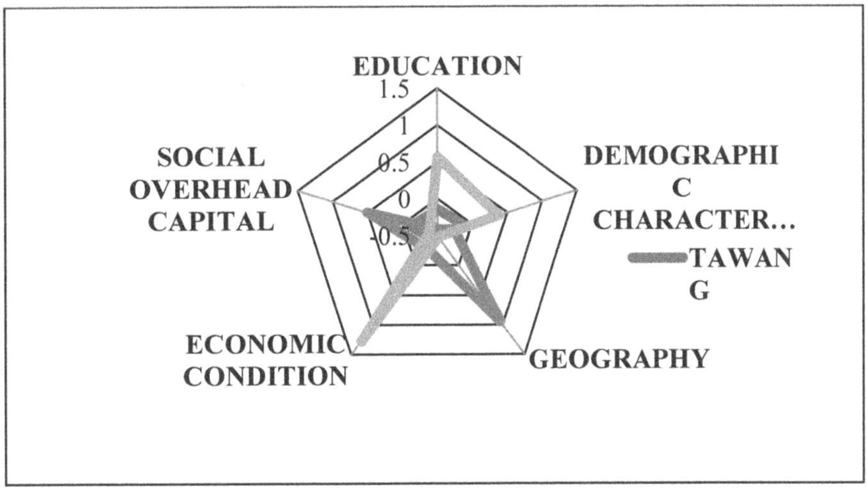

The composite Z-score is the average value computed from all the Z-scores measured for each of the variables for a given study population/individual. It provides a means for the overall assessment and thereby helps in ranking the study populations entirely based on their composite Z-score values. The composite Z-Scores of the study populations in all the five domains are comparatively shown in Figure 3. The blue line, red line and light green line represents the scores of three study populations from three districts of Arunachal Pradesh- Tawang, Papum Pare, and Tirap.

From Figure 3, it is evident that of all the study populations, the performance of the study population from Tirap is remarkably high in three out of five domains of socio-economic status namely education (composite Z-score= 0.57), demographic characteristics (composite Z-score= 0.37), and economic condition (composite Z-score= 1.28). Nevertheless, this study population is found to be the worst in comparison with other study populations in the domain of social overhead capital (composite Z-score= -0.38). Whereas, the composite Z-score of the study population from Papum Pare is found to be comparatively high in domains such as geography (composite Z-score= 0.94) and social overhead capitals (composite Z-score= 0.51). However, it is also to be noted that the performance of this population among all the study populations is found lowest in two domains- education (composite Z-score= -0.42) and demographic characteristics (composite Z-score= -0.26). As far as the performance of the study population of Tawang is concerned, this population is mostly found associated with the worst performance mainly in two domains- geography (composite Z-score= -0.47) and economic condition (composite Z-score= -0.43).

Figure 4 compares the SES of all the three study populations in terms of overall composite Z-Score. It can be noticed that the overall composite Z-scores values of the three study populations showing the level of socio-economic status range from -0.20 to 0.27 respectively.

Figure 4: Level of Socio-Economic Status (SES) of the Study Populations from Tawang, Papum Pare, and Tirap

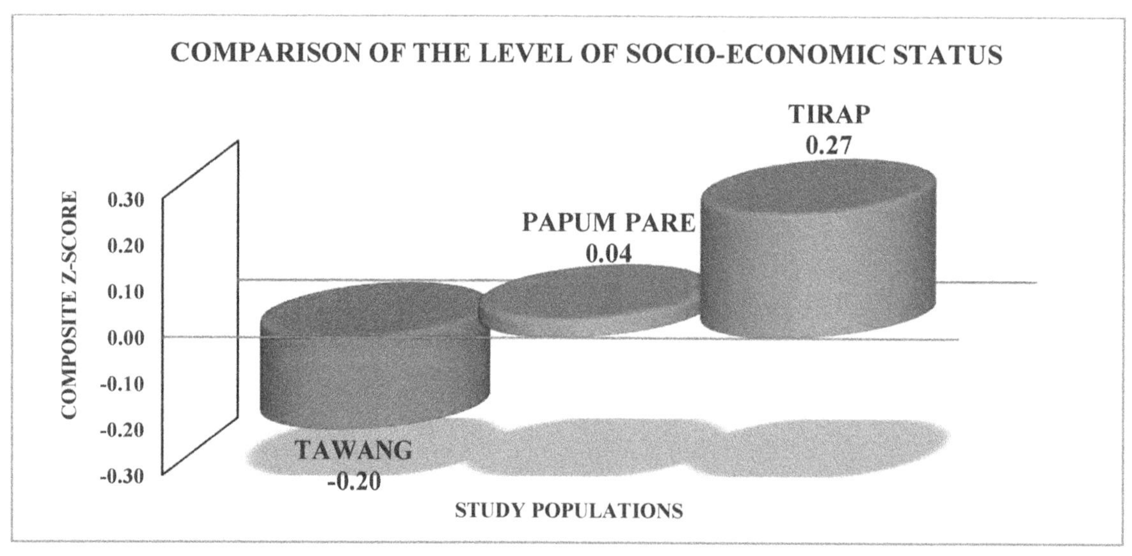

Based on the overall composite Z-score values, the following are the key findings with regards to the level of socio-economic status of the study populations:

First, the entire composite Z-score values of the three study populations fall within the plus/minus ($\pm$) first standard deviation from the mean. It implies that although the level of socio-economic status between the three study populations deviates from the mean (Z-score value= 0), however, the deviation isn't too large. For instance, the composite Z-score values could have fallen above the plus/minus ($\pm$) first standard deviation from the mean or between or above the plus/minus ($\pm$) second standard deviation from the mean respectively.

Second, although the range of all the composite Z-score values measured for the three study populations is not significantly large (0.4), still it signifies the existence of a gradient of inequality in the level of socio-economic status between the study populations.

Third, the gradient of inequality in the level of socio-economic status between the study populations can be more clearly defined by comparing the percentile rank of their socio-economic status. For instance, the composite Z-score value of the study population of Tawang is -0.20 and its corresponding percentile rank is 48th centile. It means that about 48 percent of the total observations have a socio-economic status that is below or equivalent to the level of socio-economic status of the study population of Tawang. In other words, about 52 percent of the total observations have higher socio-economic status than the study population of Tawang. Likewise, the composite Z-score value of the remaining two study populations- Papum Pare (0.04) and Tirap (0.27) shows that their corresponding percentile ranks are 51st centile and 61st centile. Now, it is easily seen that there is a wide gap between the percentile ranks of the study population, with the largest gap observed between the study populations of Tawang (48th centile) and Tirap (61st centile) and while the smallest gap between the study populations of Tawang (48th centile) and Papum Pare (51st centile). Thus, in terms of percentile rank, one can easily point out the level of disparity or inequality in the socio-economic status between study populations.

Fourth, the negative (-) and positive (+) signs of composite Z-score values also provide concrete evidence of disparity in the level of socio-economic status between the study populations.

Fifth, with regards to the disparity in the level of socio-economic status between the study populations, the highest disparity is found between study populations of Tawang and Tirap since these two populations have been found with the lowest composite Z-score value (-0.20) and highest composite Z-score value (0.27). The second-highest disparity in the level of socio-economic status can be observed between the study populations of Papum Pare and Tawang as the former is found with a composite Z-score value above the mean (0.04) while the latter with a composite Z-score value below the mean (-

0.20). And the least disparity can be seen between the study populations of Papum Pare and Tirap as both the study populations have been found with positive composite Z-score values above the mean below the first (1st) standard deviation.

Thus, it can be summarized that the overall composite-Z-score value of the two study populations- Papum Pare (0.04) and Tirap (0.27) are above the mean (Z-score= 0) while the third study population from Tawang is found with an overall composite Z-score value (-0.20) below the mean (Z-score= 0). Since a higher Z-score value is an indicator of a higher level of socio-economic status or vice versa, and hence, it can be concluded that the level of socio-economic status of the study population of Tirap (overall composite Z-score value= 0.27) is far way better than those study populations from Papum Pare (overall composite Z-score value= 0.04) and Tawang (overall composite Z-score value= -0.20).

Conclusion

Based on the key findings, three conclusions can be drawn. First, the study populations from Tirap and Tawang are found with the highest and the worst socio-economic status while, the socio-economic status of the study population from Papum Pare is comparatively good. The overall composite Z-score values measured for the study populations of Tirap, Papum Pare, and Tawang are 0.27, 0.04, and -0.20, respectively (Table 4). Since higher Z-score values with a positive sign is an indication of better socio-economic status and vice-versa, and hence, of the three study populations, the present study found the level of the socio-economic status of the two, that is, from Tirap (overall Z-score value= 0.27) and Papum Pare (overall Z-score value= 0.04), respectively, far better than the one from Tawang (overall Z-score value= -0.20).

Second, there is a gradient in the level of socio-economic status between the study populations. The level of socio-economic status of the study populations assessed with the help of Z-score statistics yielded differential Z-score values for the study populations, giving a clear indication of the existence of inequality in terms of the level of socio-economic status. The most notable disparity is found between the study populations from Tirap (overall Z-score value= 0.27) and Tawang (overall Z-score value= -0.20) while the least disparity between those from Tirap (overall Z-score value= 0.27) and Papum Pare (overall Z-score value= 0.04).

Third, the study population from Tirap completely dominated in three out of the five domains of socio-economic status while the study population from Papum Pare in two domains (**Figure 3**). On the contrary, the study population from Tawang is found mostly with poor performance in all domains. The composite Z-score values measured for the study population from Tirap are found highest in three domains of SES namely education (0.57), demographic characteristics (0.37), and economic condition (1.28). On the other hand, that of the composite Z-score values of the study population from Papum Pare is found highest in domains such as geography (0.94) and social overhead capitals (0.51).

Acknowledgement

At the outset, the authors would like to thank the esteemed Vice Chancellor (VC), Directors and Academic Officers of the three higher educational institutions- Rajiv Gandhi University (RGU), North Eastern Regional Institute of Science and Technology (NERIST), and National Institute of Technology (NIT), through whom the needful data related to total enrolled students in the academic session 2019-20 and their personal information such as name, sex, course enrolled, Gmail Address, contact number, domicile state, etc., could be gathered for the present study. Secondly, the authors are wholeheartedly grateful to every single APST student who not only showed their patience and cooperation during the telephonic interview but also for trusting the researcher with their domicile district's names. Thirdly, the authors would also like to acknowledge the contribution of the study populations (the APST students from Tawang, Papum Pare and Tirap), who indeed played the key role in the present study by responding to the online questionnaire and timely submission of the same. In addition to the above, last but not the least the contributions by Ph. D scholars namely Mr. Jyoti Saikia and Miss Manaswita Dutta are duly acknowledged and appreciated.

Reference

Adler, N. E., Boyce, T., Chesney, M. A., Cohen, S., Folkman, S., Kahn, R. L., & Syme, S. L.   (1994). Socioeconomic status and health: the challenge of the   gradient. *American psychologist*, *49*(1), 15.   Retrieved from 10.1037//0003-   066x.49.1.15

Baker, E. H. (2014). Socioeconomic status, definition. *The Wiley Blackwell encyclopedia of   health, illness,   behavior,   and   society,   2210-2214.   Retrieved from https://doi.org/10.1002/9781118410868.wbehibs395

Bradley, R. H., & Corwyn, R. F. (2002). Socioeconomic status and child   development. *Annual   review of   psychology, 53*(1), 371-399. Retrieved from DOI: 10.1146/annurev.psych.53.100901.135233

Bradley, R. (2016). Socioeconomic status. In *Encyclopedia of Mental Health: Second   Edition* (pp. 196-210).   Elsevier Inc.. Retrieved   from https://doi.org/10.1016/B978-0-12-397045-9.00223-8

Brooks-Gunn, J., & Duncan, G. J. (1997). The effects of poverty on children. *The future of   children*, 55-71.   Retrieved from https://doi.org/10.2307/1602387

Conger, R. D., Conger, K. J., & Martin, M. J. (2010). Socioeconomic status, family   processes, and individual   development. *Journal of Marriage and Family, 72*(3),   685-704.   Retrieved from DOI: 10.1111/j.1741-   3737.2010.00725.x Cowan, C. D., Hauser, R. M., Kominski, R. A., Levin, H. M., Lucas, S. R., Morgan, S. L., &

Chapman, C.   (2012). Improving the measurement of socioeconomic status for the   national assessment of educational   progress: A theoretical foundation. *National Center   for   Education Statistics*. Retrieved from https://nces.ed.gov/nationsreportcard/pdf/researchcenter/socioeconomic_factors. pdf

Cutler, D. M., Lleras-Muney, A., & Vogl, T. (2008). Socioeconomic status and health: dimensions and   mechanisms. Retrieved from DOI: 10.3386/w14333

Dutton, D. B., & Levine, S. (1989). Overview, methodological critique, and reformulation, hi   JP Bunker, DS   Gomby,   &   BH   Kehrer. *Pathways   to   Health*,   29-69.   Retrieved from https://scholar.google.com/scholar?hl=en&as_sdt=0%2C5&q=Overview%2C+ methodological+cri tique%2C+and+reformulation&btnG=

Galobardes, B., Shaw, M., Lawlor, D. A., Lynch, J. W., & Smith, G. D. (2006). Indicators of socioeconomic   position (part 1). *Journal of Epidemiology & Community   Health*, 60(1),   7-12. Retrieved   from http://dx.doi.org/10.1136/jech.2004.023531

Gupta, S., Wilejto, M., Pole, J. D., Guttmann, A., & Sung, L. (2014). Low socioeconomic   status is associated   with worse survival in children with cancer: a systematic   review. *PloS   one*, 9(2), e89482. Retrieved   from https://doi.org/10.1371/journal.pone.0089482

Hassan, U. M., & Akbar, R. A. (2020). Locus of control: Teachers' neglected attribute   towards students'   achievement scores in facing diverse socioeconomic   status. *Problems of Education in the 21st   Century*, 78(2), 282. Retrieved   from https://www.ceeol.com/search/article-detail?id=939612

Hauser, R. M., & Warren, J. R. (1997). Socioeconomic indexes for occupations: A review,   update, and   critique. *Sociological   methodology*, 27(1),   177-298.   Retrieved from https://doi.org/10.1111/1467-   9531.271028

Hoff, E., Laursen, B., & Tardif, T. (2002). Socioeconomic status and parenting. IN: MH   Bornstein (Ed) Handbook   of   Parenting   Vol.   II   (s.   161-188).   Retrieved from https://www.researchgate.net/publication/257874006_Socioeconomic_status_an   d_parenting

House, J. S. (2002).

Understanding social factors and inequalities in health: 20th century   progress   and   21st   century prospects. *Journal of health and social behavior*, 125-   142.   Retrieved   from https://doi.org/10.2307/3090192

Kahl, J. A., & Davis, J. A. (1955). A comparison of indexes of socio-economic   status. *American Sociological   Review*, 20(3), 317-325. Retrieved from   https://doi.org/10.2307/2087391

Karen, D. (1991). The politics of class, race, and gender: Access to higher education in the   United States, 1960-   1986. *American Journal of Education*, 99(2), 208-237.   Retrieved   from DOI:10.1086/443979

Lerner, R. M., Liben, L. S., & Mueller, U. (2015). *Handbook of child psychology and   developmental science, cognitive processes*. John Wiley & Sons. Retrieved   fromhttps://www.wiley.com/en-us/Handbook+of+Child+Psychology+and+Developmental+Science%2C+Volume+2%2C+Cognitive+Pr ocesses%2C+7th+Edition-p-9781118136782

Miech, R. A., & Hauser, R. M. (2001). Socioeconomic status and health at midlife: a   comparison of educational   attainment with occupation-based indicators. *Annals of   epidemiology*, 11(2),   75-84. Retrieved from DOI: 10.1016/S1047-2797(00)00079-X

Mueller, C. W., & Parcel, T. L. (1981). Measures of socioeconomic status: Alternatives and recommendations. *Child development*, 13-30. Retrieved from DOI:10.2307/1129211

Oakes, J. M., & Rossi, P. H. (2003). The measurement of SES in health research: current practice   and steps   toward a new approach. *Social science & medicine*, 56(4), 769-   784.   Retrieved   from https://doi.org/10.1016/S0277-9536(02)00073-4

Shavers, V. L. (2007). Measurement of socioeconomic status in health disparities research. *Journal of the national medical association*, *99*(9), 1013. Retrieved from https://www.ncbi.nlm.nih.gov/pmc/articles/PMC2575866/

Singh, T., Sharma, S., & Nagesh, S. (2017). Socio-economic status scales updated for 2017. *Int J Res Med Sci*, *5*(7),3264-7.Retrieved from DOI: http://dx.doi.org/10.18203/2320-6012.ijrms20173029

Sirin, S. R. (2005). Socioeconomic status and academic achievement: A meta-analytic review of research. *Review of educational research*, *75*(3), 417-453. Retrieved from https://doi.org/10.3102/00346543075003417

Solon, G., Haider, S. J., & Wooldridge, J. M. (2015). What are we weighting for?. *Journal of Human resources*, *50*(2), 301-316. Retrieved from DOI: 10.3368/jhr.50.2.301

Walpole, M. (2003). Socioeconomic status and college: How SES affects college experiences and outcomes. *The review of higher education*, *27*(1), 45-73. Retrieved from https://muse.jhu.edu/article/46608/pdf

CHAPTER 7

Spread of Covid-19 in the District of Lakhimpur, Assam

Sagir Hussain and Nishamani Kar

Abstract

The pandemic COVID-19 is the most crucial global health calamity of the century. A new infectious respiratory disease first emerged in Wuhan Hubei province China, on December 2019 in, China and was named by the WHO as COVID-19. In India, COVID-19 cases have begun towards the end of February as the case has been spiked in the month of March. In India the first case of the COVID-19 pandemic reported in the state of Kerala on 30 January 2020 and the affected had a travel history from Wuhan, China. On March 12, 2020 the first death due to COVID-19 was reported in India. This paper studied the spread of COVID-19 situation in Lakhimpur, Assam, a state of India during the year 2020. It can be said that the situation of COVID-19 spread in the district is very alarming during the months of August and September 2020 as well as in the state of Assam.

Keywords: Pandemic, infectious disease, spread, Wuhan, Calamity etc.

Introduction

The novel corona virus outbreak COVID-19 has created an unparalleled and unimaginable situation worldwide. The present catastrophic effect of the pandemic has been such that no country has ever experienced anything like this. The COVID-19 crisis is unique in the sense that it is for the first time that both economy and public health are simultaneously getting terribly affected. The spread of COVID-19 pandemic are also extraordinary and almost all countries of the world have been affected by this pandemic. The COVID-19 disease was first detected in the China, Wuhan city during the month of

December, 2019 and within this months, the disease has spread exponentially across the world. Evidently, the United States of America and those of Europe economically advanced countries have been worst affected by the pandemic. In Asia economically significant countries like China and Iran are also being affected enormously. In India, also the numbers of COVID-19 cases are increasing continuously at a worrisome rate.

All the travelers from international entering in India were asked to 14 days self-quarantine. All the States of India were asked to invoke the act of epidemic disease, which allows quarantine for suspected cases. A campaign of intensive was rolled out and guidelines were developed for surveillance, personal hygiene, contact tracing, diagnosis, quarantine, management and laboratory test. Advised people not to visit farms, where animals slaughtered places and to avoid mass gatherings. Government launched Arogya Setup app to connect the people of India for essential health services and to fight against COVID-19. Many of the schools, colleges, hotels, railway train coaches etc. were converted into facilities of quarantine.

Most countries resorted to enforce complete or partial lockdown to ensure social distancing as a measure to contain the spread of the Novel Coronavirus. Consequently, sectors like travel and communication, tourism and hospitality, trade and commerce, construction and so on, witnessed a complete paralysis. Alongside, the education sector is the one that experienced terrific challenges. The teaching–learning methodologies have been remodelled globally due to the evil outbreak that many schools and teachers around the world are struggling in alternative ways for delivery of instruction remotely **(Molise & Dube, 2020).**

In India, the Prime Minister Narendra Modi declared the first phase of nationwide lockdown of 21 days starting with 25 March 2020, which is further extended to several phases. Due to the continued lockdown, most economic activities in the country came to a halt. **(Das & Guha, 2020).**

The first case of the COVID-19 pandemic in the Indian state of Assam was reported on 31 March 2020. As of 14 March 2022 the Government of Assam has confirmed a total of 89,468 positive cases COVID-19. The state's as well as North-East largest city. Guwahati has been worst affected by Coronavirus. Assam does not provide consolidated district wise data on COVID-19, but daily media bulletins from 2020 showed most deaths were being reported from urban districts. Regarding spread of COVID-19 daily data of the total number of cumulative in India are easily available from Worldometers.info. This source of data in Assam not from the beginning it starts from 16 August onwards. Further, with high density of population, how people are well maintaining the social distance is an important point. In the initial stage of COVID-19 medical facilities to the corona patients were more readily available, but from the month of August high spread of the disease, medical facilities are getting reduced.

In Lakhimpur first Coronavirus case was detected in the town of Lakhimpur district on 4 April, the patient had attended the Conference at Nizamuddin Markaz. During the third wave of contagion, the number of COVID-19 positive cases has increased suddenly in Lakhimpur district along with the rest of the state. In this paper study the status of COVID-19 spread is concerned in the Lakhimpur district of Assam, India. We shall analyse the COVID-19 data of the spread of virus in Assam as well as in Lakhimpur district. We analysed the COVID-19 data with the help of many variables like total sample tested, positive cases, negative cases, recovery, gender wise positive cases, age wise positive cases etc.

Study Area

The study would be conducted Spread of Covid-19 in Lakhimpur District,Assam. Lakhimpur district is situated in the northern bank of the Rive Brahmaputra and the upper valley districts of Assam. The district extends between 26°49'32.23" and 27°31'24.59" north latitudes and 93°41'37.31" and 94°35'38.67" east longitudes. The district is bounded by the Papumpare and Lower Subansiri districts on the northern side, Dhemaji district of Assam is on the eastern side of the district and the river Brahmaputra and Majuli district is on the southern side. The newly divided Biswanath district (The undivided Sonitpur) is on the western side of Lakhimpur district. The geographical area of the district is 2277 sq. kms. Whereas the rural area is 2240.85 sq. kms and the urban area is 36.15 sq. km **(Census 2011).**

Objectives

1. To study the spread of Covid-19 cases in Lakhimpur district.
2. To analyses the COVID-19 cases data of the study area.

Database and Methodology

In this paper the data for the present study is collected mainly through primary and secondary sources. Similarly, visited the Karunabari and Ghilamara block for collect data from local people of COVID-19 affected area and also contact Public Health Department for secondary data. The data collected with a view to identify and analysis the Spread of COVID-19 in Lakhimpur district. Finally, data collected on different basis like: Age wise, Gender wise, total infected, total recovered, total death district and number of PCR, RDT test etc. After collection of both primary and secondary data, represent those using various visualization methods like correlation coefficient method, Line graph, Bar graph, Pie diagram etc.

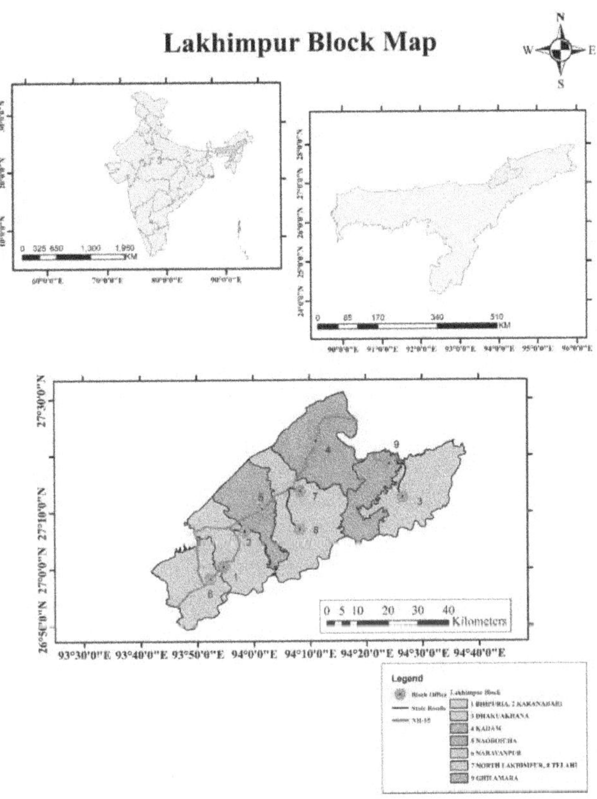

Fig 1:- Location Map of the Study Area

Outcome and Analysis

In this section presented and analyzed the COVID-19 data of Lakhimpur district, Assam. Lakhimpur lies in the Eastern part Assam which shares the boundary Arunachal Pradesh north, Dhemaji east, Majuli south and Sonitpur west. First COVID-19 case was reported in the month of April in town of Lakhimpur and after that cases tallied increasing day by day.

Tested	Numbers
Airport	1590
Railway Station-	1264

Other places-	32265
Sample Collection (RT PCR+ RAT)	152415
Positive (RTPCR+RAT)	8046
RT PCR tested	38898
RT PCR found Positive	1607
RAT tested	113517
RAT found Positive	6439

Table 1:- COVID-19 report of Lakhimpur District 2020

In the above table shows that screening for COVID-19 in the year 2020 in the airport 1590, railway stations 1264, and other places 32265. In the year 2020 Sample collection through the total RTPCR+RAT 152415 and positive cases are found 8046, RT PCR total tested 38898 and positive cases are found 1607 and finally RAT total tested 113517 and positive are found 6439.

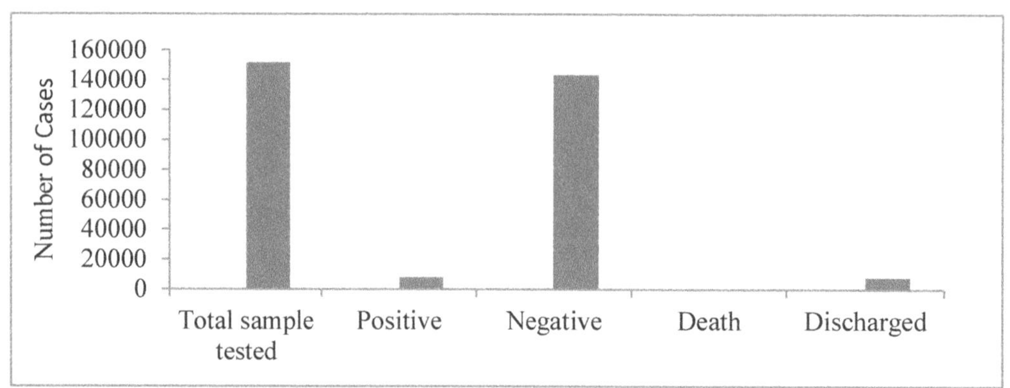

Fig 2: - Summary of COVID-19 Cases details in Lakhimpur District as on 2020

Here bar diagram shows the overall status of the COVID-19 cases in the district 2020. Out of the entire total sample tested about 15160 people 8045 positive cases and 14363 are negative cases. The recovery rate is good but not impressive as there are 10 active cases and 7976 were discharged and 59 people death.

This line graph show the age wise COVID cases of both male and female in Lakhimpur district. From the line graph we can see that the age between 25-30 are more infected because people of these age group are active, matured and they involved in different profession. They work in different places so they travelled more due to which they come in contact of different people. Hence, they are more infected. Again from the line graph we can see that age between 0-15 are not much infected. Because these age group include children, teenager who are quite safe these days in their home due to closed schools, colleges etc. Similarly, in the above line graph show that male are more infected than female. Male are much involved in outer chores like jobs, business, cultural activities so they come in contact with different people. Hence this might be the reason why we have more male infected.

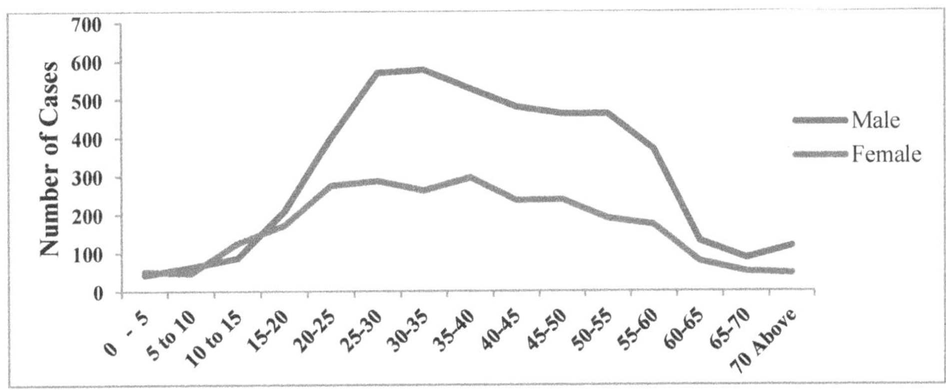

Fig 3:- Age groups and Gender wise COVID-19 cases in Lakhimpur (2020)

Result Details and Calculation of Correlation Coefficient Gender wise COVID-19 positive cases in the year (2020) of Lakhimpur District

X values
$\sum$ = 4586
Mean = 305.733
$\sum(X-Mx)^2$ = SSx = 584256.933
Y values
$\sum$ = 2528
Mean = 168.533
$\sum(Y-My)^2$ = Spy = 127613.733
X and Y Combined
N=15
$\sum(X-Mx)^2 \sum(Y-My)^2$ = 255508.133
R Calculation
$r = \sum((X - M_y)(Y - M_x)) / \sqrt{((SS_x)(SS_y))}$
$r = 255508.133 / \sqrt{((584256.933)(127613.733))}$ = 0.9357
r = 0.9357

Age Groups	Male	Female
0 - 5	43	51
5 to 10	63	47
10 to 15	86	125
15-20	209	171
20-25	400	275
25-30	570	287
30-35	577	262
35-40	528	296
40-45	480	237
45-50	462	238
50-55	462	190
55-60	370	173
60-65	131	78
65-70	87	51
70 Above	118	47

Table 2:- Age and Gender wise COVID-19 positive cases

The value of R is 0.9357
There is a strong positive correlation, which means that high X variables scores go with high Y variables scores. The value of R^2, the coefficient of determination is 0.8755

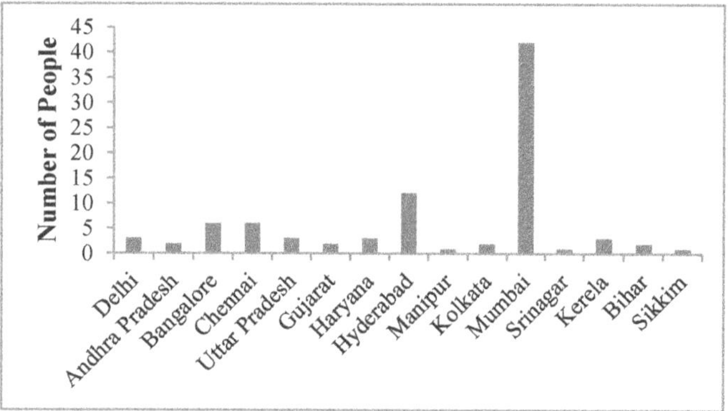

Fig 4:- Migrate from workplace to home place

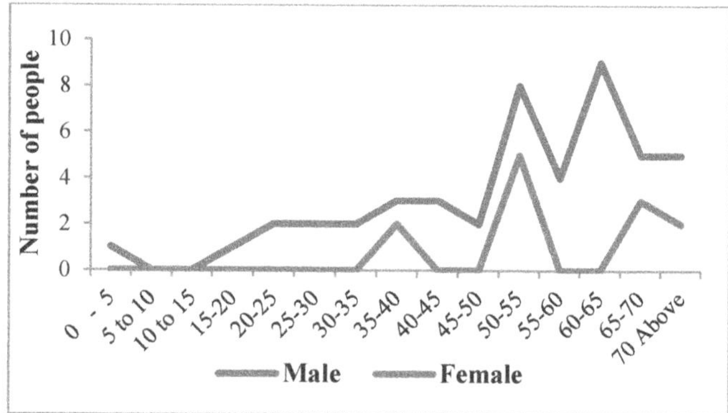

Fig 5:- Death of different sex & age groups

In the above figure 4, we can see that migrate from different states of India to Lakhimpur district during COVID-19. Total number of 89 people migrate from different states of India, maximum number of migrate came from Mumbai to home place. In the above figure 5, out of 59 people death male are 47 and female 12, maximum death of male people due their outdoor nature of work. The daily wage workers were the worst affected during lockdown, not only loss their jobs but also frustrated due to cessation of their daily income to survive. About 100 million internal migrant worker but most of them are daily wage workers who travelled out from different states of India to other states in search jobs.

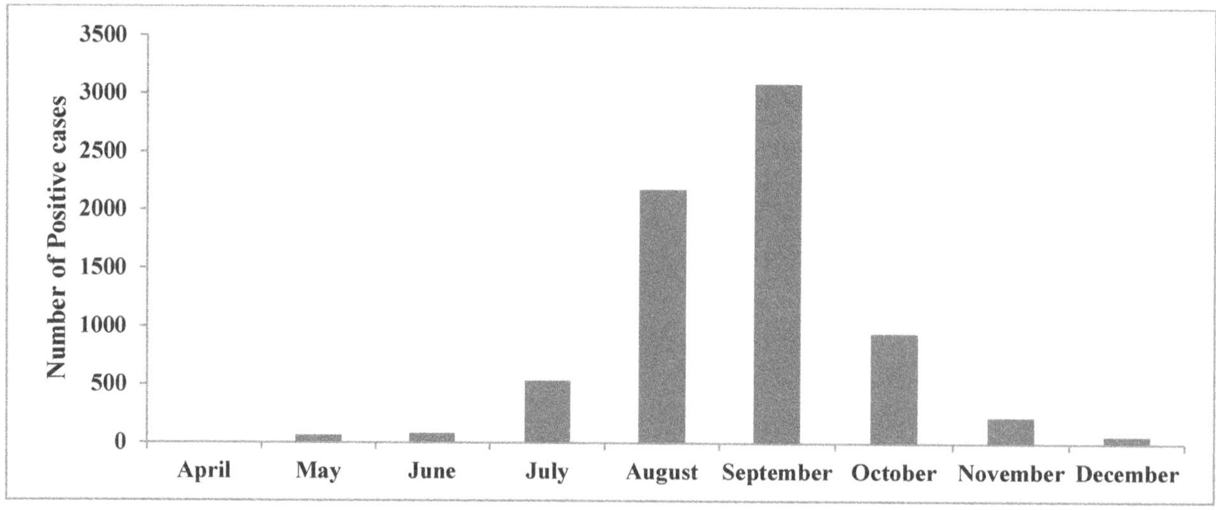

Fig 6:- Month wise number of COVID-19 positive cases

This bar graph shows the positive cases of COVID-19 in Lakhimpur district. Here we can see the bar graph the COVID-19 cases in Lakhimpur district start being detected from the month of Aril. It shows the infection number increases in exponential way starting from May to September. In the month of September largest number of positive cases (3088) recorded in the district The infected numbers of cases massive increment due to loosening of lockdown and with the reverse migrate from the work place to home district.

Findings and Results

1. First COVID-19 case was reported in the month of April.
2. Percentage of RTPCR+RAT positive cases is 5.27, RT PCR positive cases are 4.13 and RAT positive cases are 5.67.
3. Percentage of positive, negative, death and recovery comparison with total sample tested are positive cases are 5.30, negative cases are 94.69, death cases are 0.03 and recovery rate are 5.25.
4. Percentage of male and female COVID-19 cases during the year of 2020, male are 64.70 and female are 35.29. Males are more positive cases than female due to their outdoor nature of work.
5. Total 89 people migrate from other states to home place, maximum from Maharastra are 42 people
6. Percentage of death comparison with male and female, male are 79.66 and female are 20.33. Male are more death than female due to their outdoor work. According to different age groups maximum death occur between 60-65 ages.
7. Total positive case in the year 2020 in Lakhimpur district are 7162, and month wise percentage from April to December. In the month of April of only one positive case after that positive cases increasing day by day up to the month of September, May 0.83, June 1.08, July 7.40, August 30.43, September 43.11, October 13.16, November 3.08 and December 0.85.
8. Gender wise COVID-19 positive Correlation Coefficient value is 0.9357 there is a strong correlation between these two variables.

Conclusion

We have found that the situation in Lakhimpur district, as well as in Assam is very grim. The pandemic posed extensive socio-economic and health challenges and also disruption the largest economy of India. In the Indian context major reasons behind the COVID-19 pandemic identify the pitfalls in the public health care system to tackle a pandemic situation. We further highlight the citizens' role to aiding fight against this kind of pandemic by obeying government advisories of containment and social distancing. In India the reducing trend of COVID-19 cases was found to have started in the first half of May, and after that spread in the whole country is still on the increase. In Assam as well as in Lakhimpur district even after five from the start, the pandemic is still in an accelerating and unpredictable stage.

References

Baruah, H. (2020). The COVID-19 Spread in the State of Assam, The Assam Royal Global University Guwahati, Assam, India

W. Kermak, A. McKendrick, A Contribution to the Mathematical Theory of Epidemics,*Proceedings of the Royal Society A*. Vol. 115 (1927) 700 – 721. (Republished as Contributions to the Mathematical Theory of Epidemics – I, *Bulletin of the Mathematical Biology*, 53(1-2) (1991) 33-55.

COVID-19 Pandemic in Assam, en.m.wikipedia.org.

Bhatt, M. K, Thapa, J., Bhatt, B., and Mishra, K. R., (2020). Project report on status of COVID-19 in home district, Kathmandu University, Nepal

Lone, Ahmed, N., (2022). Rise and Impact of COVID-19 in India, Chandigarh University. ResearchGate

Kumar, V., and Deshwal, V., (2020), Study of Coronavirus Disease (COVID-19) Outbreak in India, Meerut Institute of Technology, 250005 Meerut, India, The Open Nursing Journal

Assam COVID-19 Dashboard, COVID-19 Advisory, Government of Assam, covid19.assam.gov.in.

Das, S,. and Kumari, R,. (2021), Statistical Analysis of COVID-19 cases in Indi, IOCER 2020, Journal of Physics: Conference Series 1797 (2021) IOP Publishing doi;10.1088/1742-6596/1797/1/012006

W. Kermak, A. McKendrick, Contributions to the Mathematical Theory of Epidemics II. The Problem of Endemicity, *Proceedings of the Royal Society A*. Vol. 138 (1932) 55 – 83. (Republished in *Bulletin of the Mathematical Biology*, 53 (1-2) (1991) 57-87.

Worldometers.info. Total corona virus cases in India, Publishing Date: September 16, 2020. Place of Publication: Dover, Delaware, U. S. A.

Hemanta K. Baruah, The COVID-19 Spread Patterns in Italy and India: A Comparison of the Current Situations, *Journal of Mathematics and Informatics,* Article in Press, Published online on July 5, 2020. (medRxiv preprint doi: https://doi.org/10.1101/2020.06.21.20136630. Posted on June 23, 2020.)

COVID-19 India. [2020-04-21]. https://www.covid19india.org/

Palash Ghosh, PhD, Rik Ghosh, MSc, and Bibhas Chakraborty, PhD (2020), COVID-19 in India: Statewise Analysis and Prediction, JMIR Public Health Surveill. 2020 Jul-Sep; 6(3): e20341. Published online 2020 Aug 12. Doi: 10/2196/20341

Dutta, P, Basu, T, and Das, A,. Spatial Analysis of COVID-19 incidence and its Determinants using Spatial Modelling: A Environmental Challenges, Volume-4, August 2021

Bhuyan. B, Borah. B and Gogoi .R, Impact of Covid-19 in the Society and Culture of Assam and its Future, European Journal of Moleculer & Clinical Medicine ISSN 2515-8260, Volume 07, Issue 09, 2020

WHO, Corona Virus Disease 2019 (COVID-19) Situation Report-15, Data as reported by National Authorities by 10 AM CET 11 March 2020

Andrews, Areekal, Rajesh K.R, Krishnan J, Suryakala R, Krishnan B, Muraly C.P, and Santosh P.V, First confirmed case of COVID-19 infection in India: A case report, Indian J Med Res 2020 May; 151(5): 490-492 doi: 10.4103/ijmr.IJMR 2131.20

Barak Bulletin, 31st March 2020 News Live, 4th April 2020 By Sentinel Digitel Desk on 16th January 2022 idronline.org

Molise H & Dube B, Emergency Online Teaching in Economic and Management Sciences Necessitated by the COVID-19 Pandemic: The Need for Healthy Relations in a Rural Schooling Context, June 2020, DOI: 10.26803/ijlter. 19.6.23

Kapoor A, Guha S, Das M K, Goswami K C & Yadav R, Digital Healthcare: The only solution for better healthcare during COVID-19 pandemic? Indian Heart Journal, Volume 72, Issue 2, March-April 2020, Pages 61-64, https://doi.org/10.1016/j.ihj.2020.04.001

Dhawan S, Online Learning: A Panacea in the Time of COVID-19 Crisis, Journal of Educational Technology Systems, First Published June 20,2020, https://doi.org/10.1177/0047239520934018

CHAPTER 8

Traditional Beads and Ornaments of the Nyishi Tribe of Arunachal Pradesh

---

Rani Cheda, Pumung Ngemu, Manngam Wangpan, and Sailajananda Saikia

Abstract

Ornaments have been a part of culture in human society since time immemorial. These ornaments are not just adornments for the body but they are symbols that distinguish a particular group of people or a community from others. These beads and ornaments are also expressions of the artistic intellect of communities. Ornaments can be regarded as the tangible expressions of any culture. The present paper is an attempt to document traditional beads and ornaments used by the Nyishi tribe of Arunachal Pradesh in North East India. The Nyishi are the largest tribal community inhabiting Arunachal Pradesh and they have a very rich culture where these traditional beads and ornaments are highly regarded. These beads and ornaments have high cultural as well as monetary value in the tribal society of the Nyishi. These beads and ornaments are part of the heirloom and a symbol of pride and prestige.

Keywords: Arunachal Pradesh, Beads, Nyishi tribe, Traditional ornaments.

Introduction

Since the beginning of human civilisation, ornaments have been a crucial part. The use of beads and ornaments of many types in daily life is strongly suggested by archaeological discoveries from ancient cultures all over the world. According to the Oxford dictionary, ornament means 'A thing used or serving to make something look more attractive but usually having no practical purpose, especially a small object such as a figurine'. Using an integration of aesthetic and utilitarian, individual and social roles, ornament represents a typology of human functions. (Glaveanu, 2014). In a simple sense, 'ornament is the art we add to art' (Trilling, 2003, p. 21). Ornaments serve a fundamental social purpose in identifying groups and communities as well as "locating" individual actors within larger, frequently geographical systems of meaning and behaviour. In this sense, ornamentsare understood to convey social information, describing the wearer to the observer and suggesting potential connections between them (Kuhn & Stiner, 2007).

The tribal people of Arunachal Pradesh love to adorn their bodies with ornaments just like people anywhere else in the globe. Their artistic sensibility and creativity are well demonstrated by these ornaments. While some of their ornaments are genuinely unique, others came from their adjacent regions of Tibet, Myanmar, Bhutan, and Assamthrough trade and barter. The people place great social, economic, and religious value on these ornaments. The origins and practices of these ornaments are rooted in a multitude of tribal folklore. Gender difference and demarcation are seen in these tribalornaments. Traditional beads and ornaments are representations of material culture in any tribal community which has been carried on for ages.

The Nyishis are one of the twenty-six major tribes of the Arunachal Pradesh. The Nyishis are the largest ethnic group of Arunachal Pradesh with a total population of about three lakhs. They largely inhabit the districts of East Kameng, some parts of West Kameng, KurungKumey, Papum Pare, KraDaadi, Kamle, Keyi Panyor, and PakkeKessang. They belong to Indo-Mongoloid group of people and their dialect belongs to the Tibeto-Burman family (Ramya and Ramjuk, 2018).

In the Nyishi community, ornaments have a great cultural significance. Ornaments are highly esteemed and regarded as symbols of social status. Some of these ornaments have high economic value and may cost thousands and lakhs of rupees. These ornaments are mandatorily exchanged as gifts during ceremonies such as weddings. The ornaments consist of various bead necklaces of different makes, head gears, armlets and bracelets, waistbands, metallic bells, cane and bamboo head gears, silver or metallic coins, shells, animal parts such as feathers, fangs, beaks, fur, and beak. One of the most interesting art forms practiced by the Nyishis is making ornaments using bell metal and lost wax techniques. This practice of bell metal casting is seen in Pichola, Nimte, and Deb villages. For the tribal artisans in these villages, bell metal craft is a major source of their livelihood.

In the Nyishi community, owning ornaments signifies pride, self-worth, and social status. An individual family's ornaments are valued possessions that can be utilised as gifts for weddings and ceremonies, or to purchase movable or immovable assets. These ornaments also act as a reserve for financial emergencies. Historically, beadswere the main goods traded in barter exchanges. The Nyishis along with some other tribal communities such as the Nah and the Tagins are known to have barter trade with Tibetans and Salt, Tibetan swords, beads of precious and semi-precious stones, coral, conch shell, and other ornaments such as brass plates and bowls, bracelets and earringswere the main commodities they acquired from the Tibetans (Menia and Amung, 2022; Bagang and Singh, 2023). These ornaments have antique value in addition to their material or financial worth. These beads and ornaments are deeply embedded in the Nyishi culture and it is an inseparable part of it.

Objectives

The primary objective of this paper is the documentation of the traditional beads and ornaments used by the Nyishi tribal community of Arunachal Pradesh with some insights into their socio-cultural significance.

Methodology

For the present study information on various beads and ornaments, their usage, cultural significance, and market value has been collected through interviews with tribal artisans involved in making ornaments, village elders, and sellers of these ornaments. Besides relevant books and other pieces of literature have been referred to for information.

Different beads and ornaments of the Nyishis

The Nyishis use several beads and ornaments. Some of these beads and ornaments are gender specific while a few of them are used by both men and women. These beads and ornaments are made of different materials such as glass, shells, plastic, cane, bamboo, and metals such as silver, aluminium, bell metal, copper, and brass. These ornaments also consist of some animal parts such as feathers and beaks. Some of these ornaments such as bell metal ornaments are locally made while many of these ornaments and beads are believed to be a product of trade and commerce between the Nyishis and other groups of people from neighbouring states and countries such as Tibet. These ornaments are of great cultural significance and they are often valued for their antiquity. Different varieties of traditional beads and ornaments of the Nyishi community are discussed in the following lines.

Sangtar

*Sangtar*is a light blue-coloured bead necklace used specifically by women. These beads are round in shape with a flat bottom and top. Generally,three to four numbers of this necklace are worn at a time. These necklaces are generally worn during festivals and marriage ceremonies. These beads are gifted to the bride by her parents during Nyishi traditional marriages. These beads are primarily used by the Nyishis of Papum Pare and KurungKumeydistricts. One single bead of *Sangter* may cost around ten thousand rupees (Chaudhuri and Chaudhuri, 2016).

Dumping

Dumping is a traditional headgear for the women folk. It is generally made up of brass metal and small blue beads. Generally, it is three to four inches wide and the numbers depend on the size of the head of the wearer. It is usually decorated with blue beads and bamboo fibres. It is generally worn during festivals and marriage ceremonies. This ornament is gifted to the bride by her parents during Nyishi traditional marriages. Generally, it is sold at a price of about five to six thousand.

Rubin

*Rubin*is an earring made of silver and circular in shape. It is exclusively worn by women during festivals and ceremonies.

Koji

Koji is a traditional metallic wrist cuff usually made of copper, silver, or aluminium. It is worn by both men and women. Unlike other ornaments, it is not exclusively worn during festivals and ceremonies but it is worn casually as well.

Hukhi

*Hukhi*is a traditional belt used by women folk that is made of bell metal. It is disc-like in shape. One single belt consists of multiple numbers of these metal discs. It is generally worn during festivals and marriage ceremonies.

Tadok

*Tadok*is a yellow-coloured bead circular in shape with a flat top and bottom. It is one of the costly beads which may cost up to eight to ten thousand rupees or more for one single bead. Cheap imitations are also available in the market which is sold at a rate of around four thousand per bead. *Tadok* is used by both men and women and is generally worn during festivals and ceremonies.

Dukli

It is a small yellow bead round and flat in shape that is used as necklaces during festivals and ceremonies. One single bead of *Dukli*may cost somewhere around rupees five hundred.

Dokming

*Dokming*is a small yellow bead round and flat in shape. Dokming necklaces are worn during festivals and ceremonies. One single bead of *Dokming*may cost somewhere around rupees three hundred.

Gaghee

It is a round-shaped copper earring exclusively for men with intricate designs on it. *Gaghee*is traditionally worn during marriage ceremonies solely.

Chungri

Chungri is a yellow-coloured bead with a round shape with a flat top and bottom. It is considered the costliest beads among all the beads used by the Nyishi tribe. One single bead may cost 20,000 rupees or even more. Possession of these beads signifies high financial status among the tribe. These beads are worn during ceremonies and festivals (Chaudhuri and Chaudhuri, 2016).

Talu

*Talu*is a large copper plate which is thick and very heavy. Its shape is similar to any regular plate but it is much larger. Though technically it is a plate it is never used for eating on it. It has great cultural significance and it is gifted to the bride by her parents in traditional Nyishi marriages. It can be considered an heirloom and due to its rarity and antiquity, it is regarded as a priced possession in the Nyishi community. Possession of this ornament is considered a symbol of prestige and financial status in the Nyishi community. A good quality *Talu* may cost around 50 to 80 thousand, while an inferior piece may be valued at around 10 thousand rupees.

Maji

*Maji*is also a type of clapper-less bell that is similar to *junghang* but it is larger and it is of a proper bell shape. Typically, it is not used as a body adornment, it is only used in rituals and kept in secret. *Maji* can be regarded as an heirloom and it is passed down from generation to generation in the Nyishi tribal society. According to popular belief, these ornaments originated in Tibet and came to the hands of the Nyishi people through trade and barter in the past. *Maji* is found in different sizes. Traditionally a large *Maji* of good make is considered to be of a value of about ten to twelve Mithuns (Bos Frontalis), which is a large bovine animal traditionally reared by the Nyishis. In terms of monetary value, it can go up to fifty to sixty lakhs approximately. It is a highly-priced possession in the Nyishi community. Its rarity and antiquity add to its value and it has cultural significance as well.

Junghang

Junghang is a conical clapper-less bell made of bell metal that is an alloy of copper and tin. They come in various sizes and the smaller ones are used as traditional body adornments by the women. They are worn crossbody and it is decorated with beads. These clapper-less belts are also used in various ceremonies and rituals. It may cost around 1500 rupees per single piece for an original one while cheap copies are available in the market for about 500 rupees.

Rinyu

It is a pair of small coin-size circular plates attached with intricate designs. It is often used with a string of blue-coloured beads called *sangmi*. It is only worn during festivals and ceremonies by the women folk across their bodies. It is valued at around rupees three hundred per piece.

TurpKoj

It is a metal wrist cuff made of bell metal generally circular with protruding designs like small mushrooms. It is only worn by men, particularly during marriage ceremonies, and by the priests or the shamans during traditional rituals and ceremonies. It is often gifted to the groom by the bride's family as a token of love during marriages.

Byopa

*Byopa*is a traditional headgear for men. It is made up of cane and bamboo strips and traditionally the upper beak of the hornbill is attached to the top. Feathers of birds such as hornbill and eagle are also attached to the headgear for adornment. In recent times due to restrictions on hunting these birds' parts such as the beak of the hornbill are made from wood and sometimes rooster's feathers are used in place of hornbill and eagle.

Conclusion

Ornament culture is an integral part of the Nyishi community. Numerous ornaments are worn during festivals and ceremonies for adornment, while some are only used in rituals. These beads and ornaments are typically gender-specific, but some of them are used by both men and women. In the tribal society of the Nyishis, these ornaments are highly regarded, symbolizing pride and financial status. The original antique pieces of these ornaments are treated as heirlooms and are valued at tens of thousands to lakhs of rupees. In recent times, many cheap machine-made copies of these ornaments have emerged in the market. Amidst the influence of modernisation, the Nyishis have very successfully kept alive their ornament culture.   As a crucial aspect of Nyishi tribal culture, these beads and ornaments must be preserved and documented.

Reference

Bagang, A., & Singh, H. V. (2023). Barter trade between the Nyishis of the undivided Subansiri area of Arunachal Pradesh with Tibet.*International Journal of Multidisciplinary Research and Development,* 10 (4), 1-4. Chaudhuri S. K., & Chaudhuri S. S. (2016). *Beads of Arunachal Pradesh: Emerging cultural context.* Niyogi Books, New Delhi.
Glăveanu, V. (2014). The function of ornaments: A cultural psychological exploration. *Culture and Psychology,* 20(1), 82-101. Doi: 10.1177/1354067X13515937

Kuhn, S. L., and Stiner, M. C. (2007). Paleolithic ornaments: Implications for cognition, demography, and identity. *Diogenes, 54* (2), 40–48. Doi: 10.1177/0392192107076870

Ramya, T., &Ramjuk, T. (2018). Changing cultural practices among the Nyishis of Arunachal Pradesh: a contextual study. *International Journal of Research and Analytical Reviews,* 5(2), 619-624.

Trilling, J. (2003). *Ornament: A modern perspective.* University of Washington Press,Seattle.

CHAPTER 9

Traditional Dress Pattern in Apatani Community of Ziro Valley, Arunachal Pradesh

Duyu Nanya and Duyu Monya

Abstract

The Apatani tribe is one of the many ethnic tribes residing in the cradle of the eastern Himalayas in the Ziro valley, Arunachal Pradesh. Dressing pattern is an important feature of all human societies. The Apatani Traditional attire is elaborate and exotic and has been handed down from generations which represent the unique handloom weaving practiced by the community. In the year 2024 these local textiles succeeded in achieving the Geographical Indication (GI) tag which stands as a showpiece of Apatani's rich cultural heritage. The following study has been conducted through using oral interviews and secondary sources to encapsulate the community's unique traditional dress pattern.

Keyword: Apatani, tanii, traditional dress, Geographical Indication.

Introduction

Climate is a fundamental factor that influence dressing pattern of a region. Throughout the course of history, individuals and families necessitated ways to protect themselves from the changing weather conditions. They were resourceful in making clothing arrangements to keep themselves warm in cold locations, to stay cool in hot regions and also stay dry in rainy seasons. Apart from the obvious function of providing warmth and protection, the clothing items also tends to serve other purposes, such as with concerning to communicating one's identity.

The mountainous Himalayan regions of the Indian Sub-continent are home to diverse groups of people, with each of them having their unique ethno-cultural traits, having been preserved mainly because of the geographical isolation. In addition, every tribe residing in a specific region have its characteristics traditional dress and costume. These regional costumes or dressing pattern that are associated with a specific location, geographic area or a certain period of time in history expresses an 'identity.' It can also be done in practise to indicate one's social, marital or religious status. The costume that is used to represent the identity, culture or ethnicity of a group, is known as ethnic wear, traditional dress or local costumes. These costumes often do come in two forms i.e. one for everyday wear/formal wear and the other for traditional occasions/ festivals.

Arunachal Pradesh has an exotic plethora of socio-cultural life that smoothly blends different types of lifestyles, cultures and traditions. Ethnic shawls, body wraps (*gale*) and *lungis* are the fashion favourites here. With as many as 26 major distinct tribes and over 100 sub-tribes, the state of Arunachal Pradesh is a visual treat for those population who are genuinely interested and involved in a glimpse of a cultural diversity. Basically being a tribal state, local festivals and social events like child births, weddings etc are an integral part in the lives of people here. The major tribes of the state include Nyishi, Adi, Apatani, Galo, Tagins, Monpa, Sherdukpens, Aka, Mishmi, Nocte, Tangsa, Bori, Bokar, Singphos etc. Whilst most of the tribes are ethnically similar, having being derived from the same ancestors, but their geographical separation has brought in the difference in the pattern of their dressing styles.

The Apatani tribe's traditional dresses are colourful and attractive, yet simple in style. In the olden days, the Apatanis (*taniis*) had gained an immense local reputation for being able to produce clothes of particularly high quality and elaborate patterns.

Study Area

Ziro Valley of Lower Subansiri District in Arunachal Pradesh is located at the geographical extent of 27.63°N and 93.83°E at an altitude of about 1688 metres to 2438 metres. The area is characterized by cold, humid, subtropical and temperate types of climate with relative humidity remaining constant between 70-80%. The valley covers an area of about 147.44 Km² and is drained by the *Kiile* River which runs longitudinally in the north-south direction. Numerous streams and gullies from east to west join it and drain the area. The Ziro valley was initially a swampy wasteland. The Apatanis are said to have settled down in Talley Valley (about 25 km south-east from Ziro town) for sometime before relocating their base to Ziro (Haimendorf, 1962). The Apatani tribe are one among the major tribes in Arunachal Pradesh with a total population of 43, 777 as per India Census, 2011 dwelling in 6 different villages of the valley viz. *Hari, Bulla, Hong, Hija, Dutta* and *Bamin-Michi*.

Figure 1. Location Map of Study Area

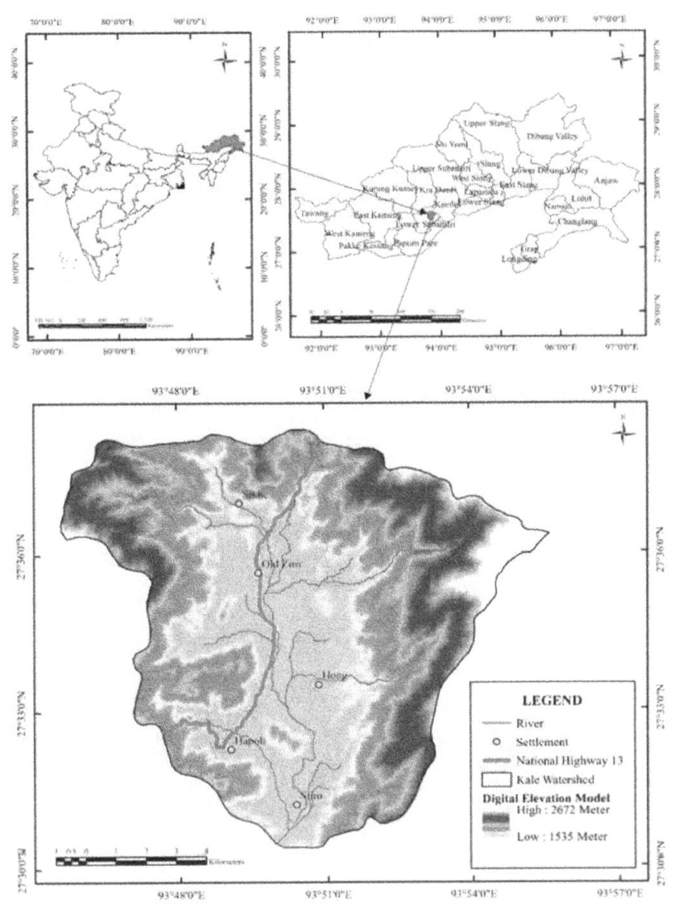

(Source: Downloaded from https://bhuvan.nrsc.gov.in and Generated Using ArcGIS 10.3 software)

Data Base and Methodology

For the present study, both primary data and secondary data have been considered.

- The primary data has been collected during the survey through oral interview.
- Information from secondary sources is very much essential for framing the theoretical background of the study area. Therefore, the secondary data has been collected from various official sources such as Census Report of India, District Statistical Handbook of Lower Subansiri district, Books, Research Journals, articles, documents etc.

Oral interview was conducted with the concerned respondents regarding the areas of inquiry for this research. With the collection of information and data, photographs were also taken for documentation purpose. The photographs are shown in the form of figures in this study.

Findings and Discussions

Traditionally, the Apatani men tied their hair in a knot just above the forehead (*piiding*) by using a brass rod (*piiding kotu*) placed horizontally which measured 12 inches in its length. The men used to tattoo their chin (*tiippe*) in the shape of a 'T' below the lower lip. The art of practising tattooing and the stuffing of large nose plugs (*Yaping hullo*), which was once very popular among the Apatani women of the Ziro valley has gradually declined in the recent years (Figure 2). That practice had reportedly started because the Apatani women wanted to look unattractive to males from the neighbouring tribes. The Indian Government during the 1970s banned the use of nose plugs as it made the Apatani women easily recognizable and prone to discrimination *(Source: Indiatimes.in)*

Figure 2. An Apatani Woman and Man
(*Source: arunachallivingheritage.com*)

Figure 3. Daily wear of the *taniis* in earlier days
(*source: arunachallivingheritage.com*)

Colour is an important aspect determining the dressing pattern for ceremonial duties. Colours that dominate the Apatani fabrics are red, yellow, dark blue, orange and blue. Red shade (either flame or dark red) in particular, is the most dominant colour of most female ceremonial attire. In the past decades, colours for weaving Were obtained by using a variety of plant dyes from plant species such as *tamin* (*Rubia cordifolia*) for getting red/orange colour and *sankhii* for getting yellow/brown colour. Indigo blue was the central colour of many male ceremonial garments which was sourced from a wild plant *Yango*. As the process of manual colouring is long and tedious, as of today, most of the organic dyes have been replaced by synthetic ones.

In the early days, the range and choice of handloom products for daily use was limited in case of both men and women. During that time, most of the local wears were weaved in various shades of the basic beige, whitish or cream colour. Men customarily used to wear a thick short sleeves cotton jacket (*jikhe tarii*) with a type of loincloth (*sarbe*). The women used to wear a similar jacket (*kente tarii*) as that of their male counterpart along with a black and white skirt, which was called as *kente abi* (Figure 3). In addition, the male and female used to wrap themselves by a coarse cotton shawls called as *kente pulye*.

Figure 4. Apatani women adorned by *Jilya Pulye*
(*Source: arunachallivingheritage.com*)

During the coldest months of the year the *tanii* people used to cover their body with thick home-made woollen coats (*tongo*). The wool material was never produced by the Apatani communities living in the valley but was always bartered or bought from outside the valley. Apatani people's another popular coat (*Jilya pulye*), made out of coarse silk was also obtained from outside (Figure 4). *Jilya Pulye* can be worn by folding it into two parts and then wrapping it around the body (left side), with two ends diagonally being tied across one shoulder (right side).

Gaale (cloth piece used as lower wrap) and skirts for festive or local occasion tend to bear more complex and intricate patterns and are very colourful in its look. *Supun tarii* (shirt) and *Bilan abi* (skirt) makes for the traditional attire during the Myoko Festival of the Apatanis.

Figure 5. *Bilan Abi*: A ceremonial skirt

Figure 6. Chinyu Abi: A casual Apatani skirt

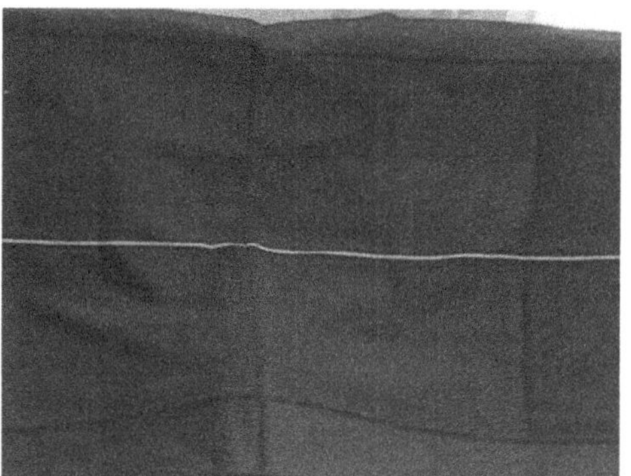

Figure 7. Bilan Abi: A ceremonial skirt

Figure 8. Pissa Lenda Abi: A unique and exotic ceremonial Skirt

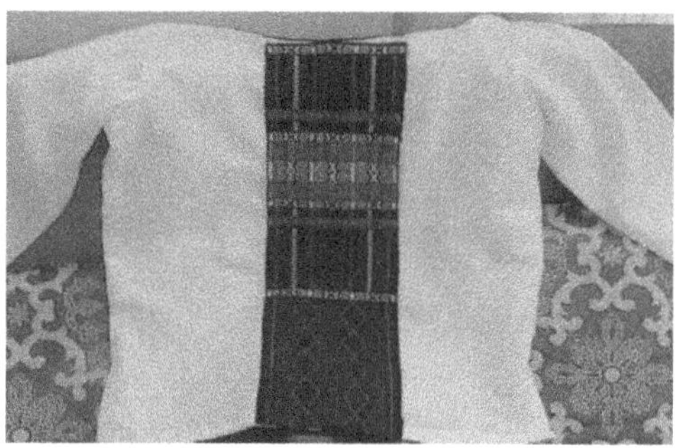

Figure 9. Supun tarii: A ceremonial Shirt

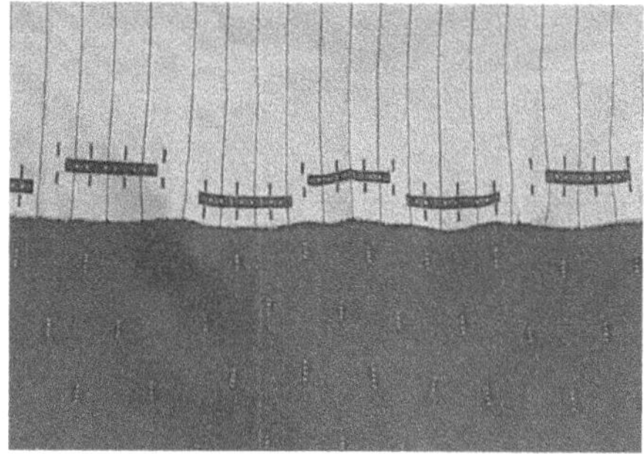

Figure 10. Bilan Abi: A ceremonial skirt

Jig-Jiro and *Jilan* shawls are majorly used by the common and general *tanii* people during collective ceremonies such as *subu tanii, supung, penii, mida, murung,* etc. These days, the modern versions of *Jilan*, which are mostly without motifs, are being manufactured and sold for such purposes. However, the decorated type of *Jilan* is not being used in daily lives and is spared only for important ceremonial occasions. As per the study by the anthropologist F. Haimendorf, *tanii* shawls such as *Jig-Jiro* and *Jilan* used to fetch good prices among their neighbouring tribes and were hugely bartered in a direct or indirect way.

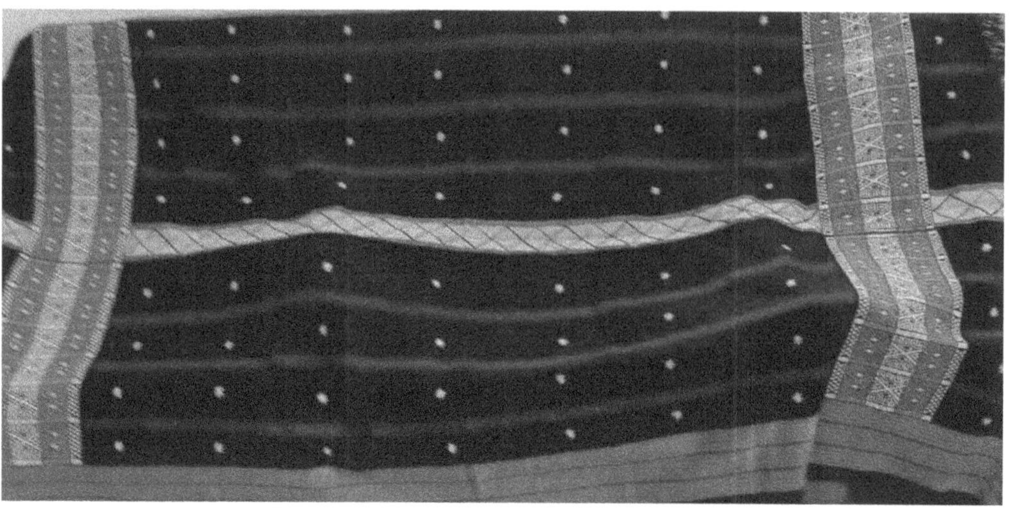

Figure 11. *Jilan Pulye*: The priestly shawl which is the most expensive piece of ceremonial Apatani costume

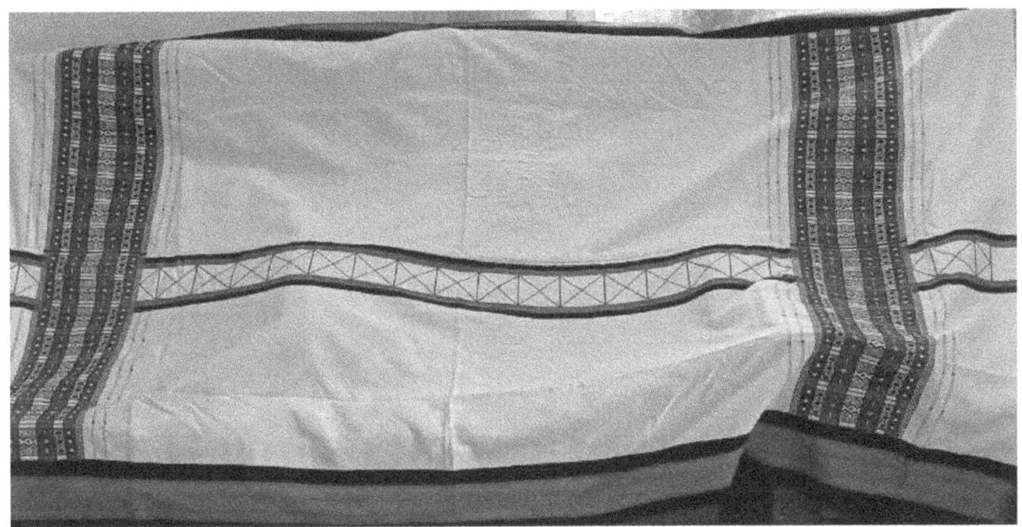

Figure 12. Pyamin Pulye: The traditional shawl used by the commoners during ceremonial festival

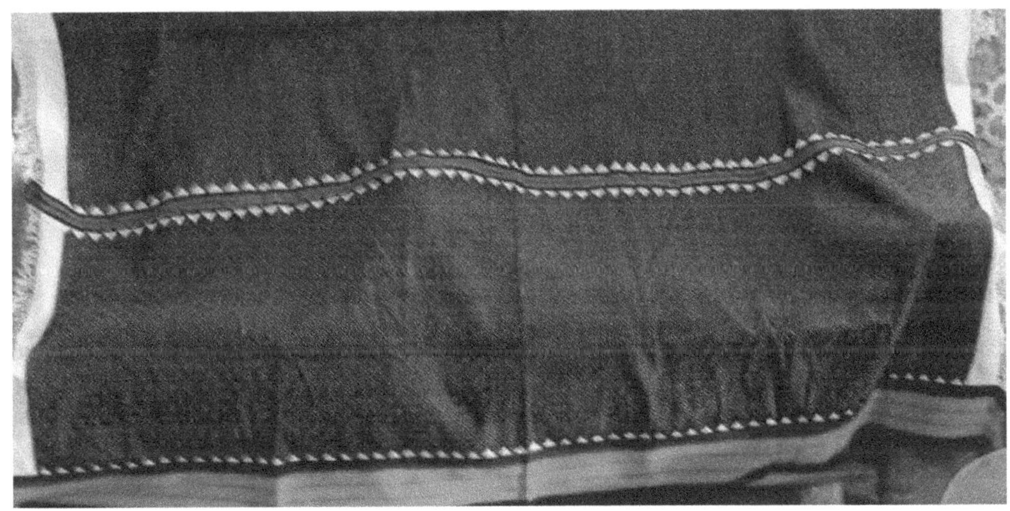

Figure 13. *Jiikhe Pulye*: An exotic ceremonial Apatani shawl

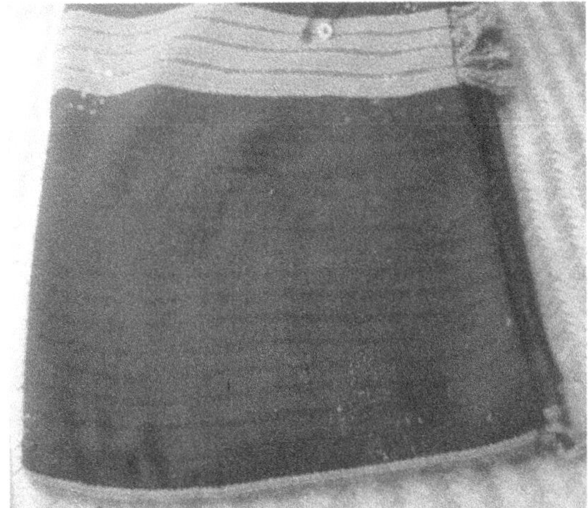

Figure 14. *Zig Ziro*: The precious Apatani shawl of an adjudicator and a priest

Ornaments consisting of beads made of metals, precious stones, elephant's tusk, some wild animal's teeth etc forms a very important and significant part of the Apatani's traditional wear. *Sampu* (white), *lebu* (red) *liirin* (grey), *sanpyu* (blue) *tado* (yellow) *bimpu* (dark blue) are the prominent necklaces worn by the Apatanis during ceremonial functions. The different types of bangles includes, *rupu kobyan* (right side bangle) *nyiime kori kobyan* (left side bangle), *ami kobyan* and *kop kobyan.*

Figure 15. Traditional wear of the Apatani priest when performing local rituals

Figure 16. An Apatani Couple adorned with Ornaments during Myoko festival

Conclusion

Two or three generations back, the Apatani Textiles were known for its good quality, as all clothing materials used to be weaved on the traditional bamboo looms at home. But now a day, most of the handloom products consist of only ceremonial dresses. Except for the priestly attire, much of the festive and ceremonial materials can now be brought from private enterprises or government emporiums. Thus, it is to be said that the craft of traditional home weaving is being slowly forgotten by the valley people, although a few are still trying to preserve it to date.

Although the facets of urbanization and modernity is gradually engulfing the lives of the people of Ziro Valley, the clothing styles and designs have largely been uninfluenced and *tanii* people still practises to wear their local/traditional/ethnic costumes for ceremonial functions and ritiuals. However, there has also been a small scale inspirations in forms of motifs that have made their advancement into the Apatani clothing design. The Apatani fabric is widely recognized for its geometric and zigzag patterns, along with its angular designs. During the year 2021 an application seeking a Geographical Indication (GI) tag for the Arunachal Pradesh Apatani textile product was filed by Zeet Zeero Producer

Company Limited. The Chennai (Tamil Nadu) based Geographical Indication (GI) Registry in 2024 awarded the GI tag to 12 distinctive products from Arunachal Pradesh, among which, was also included the Apatani Textile. This achievement stands as a testament of the rich cultural heritage and traditional craftsmen ship embedded within the heart of the Apatani community and reflects a dedication in preserving their traditional way of life.

Reference

Census of India. (2011). *District wise Scheduled Tribe Population*. Office of the Registrar General & Census Commissioner, India District Statistical Officer. (2014).

District Statistical Hand Book of Lower Subansiri District. District Statistical Office, Lower Subansiri Distict, Ziro

Dutta, Srishti B. (2023). Face tattoos, Nose Plugs: This is how Apatani Women Prevented Abductions from Tribal Raiders. https://www.indiatimes.com

Haimendorf, Christoph V F. (1962). Apa tanis and Their Neighbours: A Primitive Society of the Eastern Himalaya

Konwar S, Boruah S and Kalita B. (2020). Academic and Law Serials Traditional Dresses of Apatani Tribe of Arunachal Pradesh

https://www.arunachallivingheritage.com

https://www.savetanii.blogspot.com.au

CHAPTER **10**

Structure of Rural life and Sustainability of Phuhuratali Char Village of Sipajhar Community Development Block in Darrang District, Assam

Chitra Rani Barua

ABSTRACT

Environment plays an important role to develop the economy of a nation. The availability of natural resources will accelerate the development of a place if we used the resources with proper way. But in present day situation the overexploitation of natural resources which is threatening to the future generation. Darrang is an important agrarian district of Assam. The entire economy of the district depends on agriculture. The char dwellers of Darrang district are very hard working population. They depend on agriculture to sustain their life in this area. In this area the dwellers practices different types of crop in season wise. Due to the frequent flood in this area it is not possible to practice agriculture whole year. Sustainability of char dwellers that how they are to sustain themselves in this area, what are the economic conditions of the people of this area? Keeping this point of view, the researcher considers it important to undertake an analytical study on Structure of rural life and sustainability of Phuhuratali village of sipajhar community development block of Darrang district, Assam.

Key words: Char, Darrang, Environment, Sustainability, Rural

INTRODUCTION

The environment is defined as the sum total of all conditions and influences that affect the development organism (Gautam, 2013). Environment can be defined as a sum total of all living and non-living elements and their effects that influence on human life. The environment provides the supply of available resource sustains life by providing genetic and biodiversity and enhances the quality of life. Environment plays an important role to develop the economy of a nation. The availability of natural resource is supposed to accelerate the development of a place if we used the resources with proper way. But in present day situation the overexploitation of natural resources which is threatening to the future generation.

Sustainable development is development that meets the needs of the present without comprising the ability of future generations to meet their own needs (UN World Commission), Sustainability is the balance between the environment, equity and economy. The integration of environmental health, social equity and economic vitality are the basic elements of sustainability which create an environment on thriving, healthy, diverse and resilient communities for this generation and generations to come. The sustainability presumes that resources are finite, and should be used conservatively and wisely with a view to long-term priorities and consequences of the ways in which resources are used (Sustainable committee, UCLA). Now a day the word 'sustainability' is widely used by all development theories. The concept of sustainability has a long historical background. In the period of Rigvedic the nature act a prominent role as a controller of all the human activities.(Gautam,2013).

Location of the study Area:

The word "Sipajhar" is derived from two terms the 'Sipha' referring to an ancient river passing through this area and the 'Jhar' to the woods grown on the bank of the river and eventually which come to known as Sipajhar. The area is extends latitudinally from 26°12′42″ to 26°32′25″ and longitudinally from 91°44′49″ to 91°57′18″. It is located in the middle part of the Brahmaputra valley of and is surrounded by river Saktola in the east, Barnadi in the west, Mangaldai-Majikushi Road in the north and the mighty Brahmaputra river in the south. The study area in this paper focus on the char village of phuhuratali of Sipajhar community development blocks in Darrang distrct. Phuhuratali village is located in Sipajhar community development of block of Darrang district. Geographical area of this village is 563.2 hectares with total population 4370 according to 2011. It is situated 45 km away from the district headquarter Mangaldai. And it is 5 to 10 km from Sipjhar. Bazana Pathar is the gaon Panchayat of Phuhuratali village. In the study from this village taking 192 (at least 30 percent) household from total household 640.

The main occupation of the people in this village is agriculture. Due to the frequent flood the farmer of this village are practices Rabi crops instead of Kharif crops. Basically the farmers cultivated the summer rice. From the study it is found that the farmers are interested to cultivate the maize instead of jute because of the market benefits. The people of this village are spent a very natural rural life. The livelihood pattern of this village is very simple and it is connected to natural resources. They maintain an eco-friendly relationship with nature. They preserve natural setting because they must know that nature is the main source of income. Although they have no any knowledge about the sustainability but they maintain automatically a sustainable life.

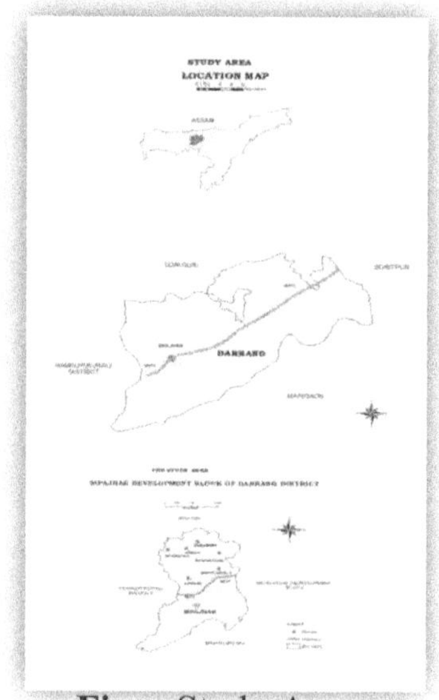

Fig: - Study Area

Objectives of the study:

The objectives of the study are

1. To study the economic conditions of the study area
2. To study the rural life structure in the study area.

Methodology of the study:

The data for the present study have been collected through intensive field work which were carried out in the study area in several ways. The data for proposed study includes both primary and secondary data. Undertaking field work, library work was undertaken primarily in departmental library of the Gauhati University. The secondary source materials were also collected from census records, Char development office of Darrang District, land revenue reports, settlement group reports and other documents. The field data are collected through the questionnaire.

Result and Discussion:

Darrang is an important agrarian district of Assam. About 85 percent of population is engaged in agriculture. The entire economy of the district depends on agriculture. The soil of Darrang district is very fertile and it is very suitable for agricultural production. The char dwellers of Darrang district are very hard working population. They depend on agriculture to sustain their life in this area. In this area the dwellers practices different types crop in season wise. Due to the frequent flood in this area it is not possible to practice agriculture whole year. So the farmers of char areas of Darrang district is interested practices some commercially benefited crop like maize. Few years ago, the char dwellers are practices largely the jute cultivation. But the demand of jute declined due to the frequent flood. So the farmers are interested to practices maize instead of jute. The marketing value is very sound in maize cultivation. The people of char areas are practices the other crops also such as different types of vegetables, pulses, gram, potato, sugarcane etc. Here, discuss about the sustainability of char dwellers that how they are to sustain themselves in this areas, In this regard selected a village named Phuhuratali of Sipajhar community development block in Darrang district.

Population Structure of the Representative Village:

In this village, there are 123 male and 100 female population are found in the age group of 0-6. The working populations are found 309 male and 298 female in the age group of 15-59 years. From the selected household the total population is found 1155. Out of this 29.78 percent male population are literate in this village. It is very low. The female literacy is quite high than the male literacy it is 30.38 percent. The education system is not sound. The people of this village are not aware about education.

Occupational structure of the Representative Villages:

The occupational structure of a region is defined by the segment of a region, population that engaged in economic ventures and various professions. Occupational structure plays a vital role to improve the economy of a region. And simply the occupation is defined the principal work or business which the person carries out on daily basis to earn their primary earning. The economy of Darrang district is primarily agricultural in nature. The other crops which are in practice in the area by the farmer like wheat, mustard, pulses, maize, jute, and different types of vegetables. The dwellers of this area is very hard working. Men as well as female population are engaged in agricultural sectors. They practice different types of crops in their agricultural field. But due to the changing of time the occupational structure is quite change in this region. Now a day, the char dwellers are interested in animal husbandry. Livestock is second important occupation of rural population. In this agrarian region livestock plays an important role improve economic level of the area. The following table no.1 shows the occupational structure of village phuhuratali.

Table 1 Occupational Structure of Phuhuratali Village of Sipajhar Community Development Block

Sl. No.	Occupation	Population
1	Agriculture	725
2	Business	40
3	Animal husbandry	6
4	Service	5
5	Others	10
6	Productive Population	788

Source: Calculated on basis of primary data collected from the field

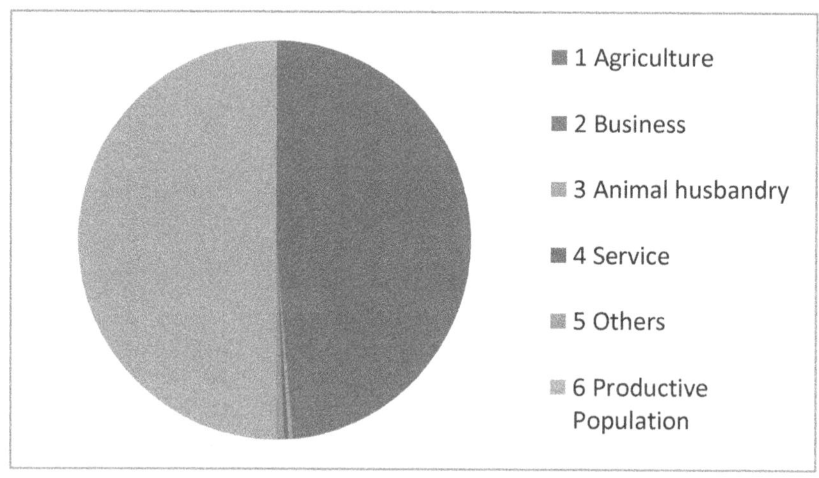

Fig. Occupational structure of the village

From the Study occupation of this village, which is shown in the table no. 2, it is found that the majority of the population are engaged in agriculture. There are 725 numbers of population in Phuhuratali village earn their income from agriculture. Thus, the area is dominated by agriculture. The major source of livelihood of the study area is agriculture. There are 40 numbers of populations who are engaged in business in this village. It is to be say that the occupational structure of this area is changing due to the increase of population and also demand of time. Besides some people are engaged in teaching job, advocates, private job etc.

In the present day situation the char area people are interested in rearing animals in business purpose. Basically the cattle and goat are main domestic animals for most of the household in this village. In Phuhuratali village of Sipajhar development rearing buffalo, cow and poultry. Because some families are earn their income through this. With 53.57 percent of population Phuhuratali village of

Sipajhar community development block has occupied livestock. Cows are reared by 15 numbers of households in this village. Buffalo, goat, sheep are reared by the 10 numbers, 25 numbers, and 5 numbers of households respectively. There are 80 numbers (31.74 percent) households have poultry.

Agricultural Structure of the Village:

Almost all the char areas of Darrang district are now inhabited by the immigrant Muslim. As agriculture is found the major source of livelihood in the study area. The agricultural activity of this area is rain fed. The char area is very flood prone area. Due to the frequent flood there is not possible to practices all types of crops in a year. The people of this village are constantly practicing cultivated the Rabi crops. But in changing of time and use of modern equipments like, tractor shallow tube well, solar power pump, the farmers are practice the Ahu rice and Boro rice and a small portion of Sali rice. They practice different types of vegetables, maize, sugarcane in their crop field. In the following table no. 2 attempt is made to examine the purpose of agricultural production produced by the farmers. Due to the frequent flood the farmers are practice summer rice in this village.

Table: 2 Production of Major Crops in the village

Total Cropped Area	Production of Major Crops(in quintal)										
	Summer rice	Winter rice	Autumn rice	Maize	Pulses	Wheat	Rap & Mustard	Vegetable	Jute	Potato	Sugarcane
72.57	525.25	--	12	1815.01	-	--	125.9	712	-	128	25.1

Source: Calculated on the basis of primary data collected from the field

The agricultural productivity is affected by the availability of irrigation facilities. The irrigation facility is not so good in this village. The farmers are still dependent on weather condition and the season for agricultural farming. In the study, it is found that the farmers of this village are used tube well for irrigation. A new technology of irrigation solar power pump or solar with shallow motor used in the crop field in this village although it is not sufficient for growing production level. From the field observation the farmers of this village used the solar motor pump with taking loan and some of them used by the BPL solar motor in their crop fields. A few numbers of farmers are using the canal for irrigation. From the field study it is found that the production summer rice and autumn rice are 525.25 quintal and 12 quintal in a year respectively. The maize cultivation very high in this village which is 1815.01 quintal. The farmers are interested to cultivate maize instead of jute in the present time.

Use of fertilizer in this area is not sufficient and not used in proper scientific way. In the study it is found that most of the farmers are use fertilizers in the agricultural production. Most of the farmers are uneducated and it affects the utilization of fertilizers in the agricultural production. All the farmers use the fertilizers as directed by the seller.

Structure of Houses in the Village:

The present study has examined the types of houses of this representative village. From field observation it is found that the people of char area use the *kuccha* houses. The following table no. 3reveals that the house types possessed by the villagers of the study area.

Table: 3 Types of House in the village

Types of Houses	Phuhuratali	
	No. of Household	%
Kuccha	158	82.29
Semi Pucca	25	13.02
Pucca	9	4.68
Total	192	

Source: calculated on the basis of primary data collected from the field

In the table it is found that the house types of the village are *kuccha* houses. Among them some have built the *semi pucca* (13.02 percent) and *pucca*(4.68 percent) houses. It is found that out of the total household numbers 82.39 percent of *kuccha* house types in Phuhuratali.

The standard of house types of the study area is minimum standard. Basically the people of char areas use the bamboo, paddy straw, jute stick, leaves, mud etc for their house materials. Some of them are use the wood or galvanized sheet. Among them some people of this area are built their houses with concrete materials and galvanized roof. Due to the heavy flood the people of the char area use the galvanized sheet as house wall. From the field observation it is found that the people of Phuhuratali village of Sipajhar community development Block use the alluvial soil as cement for their house floor.

Sources of Drinking Water in the Village:

The sources of drinking water in the study area all villages are used the tube-well for their sources of drinking water. Some of the households in the study area use river water for other purposes and also sometimes for households consumption purposes. From the study it found that 93.75 percent of households of Phuhuratali village are using own tube-well for their source of drinking water and other household consumption but 6.25 percent do not have the own sources of drinking water in this village. So they collect the drinking water from their neighbours. Although most of the households have their own tube-well and using the water for drinking and other household consumption but many of them have said that the drinking water is not pure.

Sources of Cooking Fuel in the Village:

For cooking fuel, the people of Phuhuratali village of Sipajhar Community Development Block has used the different thing like, dry cow-dung, fuel-wood, paddy-straw, jute stick, kerosene, liquid petroleum gas(LPG) etc. From the field study it is found (table no.4) that fuel-wood used in the Phuhuratali village of Sipajhar community development block is very high it is 115 numbers (59.89 percent) of households. There are 55 numbers (28.64 percent) of household use the cow dung, fuel wood, paddy straw as their cooking fuel. Only 7 numbers (3.64 percent) of household use the fuel wood and LPG for their cooking purpose.

Table: 4 Sources of Cooking-Fuel in Representative Village

Total No. of Surveyed Households	Fuel-wood		Cow-dung, Fuel-wood, Paddy-straw		Cow-dung, Fuel-wood, Paddy-straw, LPG		Fuel-wood, LPG	
	Nos.	%	Nos.	%	Nos.	%	Nos.	%
192	115	59.89	55	28.64	15	7.81	7	3.64

Source: Calculated on the basis of primary data collected from the field

Sanitation Facilities in the village:

The sanitation facility of the study area is not very good quality. In the field study majority of the people are use *kuccha* toilet. The distribution of toilet types owned by the people households of representative villages are classified as *Kuccha, semi-pucca*, and *pucca*. In the following table no.5 is presented the types of toilet using by the people of the village. Phuhuratali village of Sipajhar Community Development Block's 91.14 percent households use the *kuccha* toilet. In Phuhuratali village of Sipajhar Community Development Block it is only 6.25 percent and only 2.60 percent households are use the pucca toilet.

Table: 5 kinds of Toilet owned by the village

Kinds of Toilet	Phuhuratali	
	Nos.	%
Kuccha	175	91.14
Semi-pucca	12	6.25
Pucca	5	2.60
Total	192	

Source: Collected from the field study

Market Facilities in the village:

The market facilities of the study area is not very sound. They highly use the local market to sold their different types of finish products such weekly market and daily market. The people of the Phuhuratali village are marketing in the near weekly and daily market Garukhuti, Dhanbari and some of them are coming to Dumunichowki and Sipajhar also.

Transport and Communication Facilities of the Village:

In the study area the transportation facility is not good one. The road connectivity is very poor in the study area. In summer season they faced a terrific situation on transport. That time they use the motor boat (locally known as Bhutbhuti). In winter season day use motor bike, bullock cart, boat, etc.

From the above analysis, the following findings are come out:

1. The people of the char area is not understand the environmental problems and pollution. They have not any idea about the sustainability. Although they maintain a eco-friendly relationship with the environment and perform a sustainable life automatically.
2. The source of economy of the study area is depend on agriculture. But it is not sufficient for their livelihood. So the people of the study area are engaged another activities also. The agricultural system is traditional method. The most of farmers are not effort the modern equipments in their field. Some of them are using chemical fertilizers in their crop field but it is unscientifically.

3. In the study area less deforestation is seen. They preserve natural resources because they know that the nature is the main sources of income.

4. In the changing of time the literacy rate of the study area is quite high but quality of the educated people not satisfactory. Majority of population are illiterate in the study area. The income source of the study area is based on agriculture. Agriculture is the backbone of the char areas of Darrang district. But the area is affected by natural calamities especially flood in every year so the production of agriculture is very low. The use of modern techniques is very low.

5. From the it is found that the households of the study area are use the natural resources for cooking maximum. The fuel-wood is very usable cooking fuel in the study area.

6. The char area is geographically isolated from the mainland areas. The main source of communication between the char areas and main land areas is boat.

Conclusion:

In the study area the rural economy is based on agriculture and the source of economy also agriculture and nature based. Lake of proper education the people of this area is unable to use modern techniques in their crop field. They have no any knowledge about sustainability although they preserve their nature, because they know that the main sources of earning is the nature.

References:

Chakraborty, G (2006): Assam Hinternalds: Society and Economy in the Char Areas of Assam (New Delhi: Akansha Publishing House)

Das, M.M. (2012); 'Peasant Agriculture In Assam' a Structural Analysis, Published by eastern Book house, Guwahati, India

Deka, N (2012): agro-Ecosytem in the Brahmaputra valley, Assam, Dynamics and sustainability, PhD Thesis, Department of Geography, Gauhati University

District Census Hand Book, 2011

Gopal Krishnan, R (2000): assam Land and People, published by R.Kumar Omsons Publications, New Delhi

Khandakar,Abdullah (2016): Social Exclusion of Inhabitants of Char : A study of Dhuburi District in Assam, Phd. Thesis, Sikkim University

Nath, L. (2005): Darrang District Through Ages, Published by Karuna Medhi, Dhekiajuli, Sonitpur, Assam

Saxena, H.M. (2004): Environmental Geography, Rawat publications, Jawaharnagar, Jaipur

Singh,Savindra (2010): Environmental Geography, Prayag Pustak bhawan, Allahabad

Sarma,M & Saikia,C (2020): Status of Vegetable Farming and its Challenges in Central Brahmaputra Floodplain Environment of Darrang District. International Journal of Advanced Research in Engineering and Technology, vol.11, Issue 10, pp 1503-1514, http://iaeme.com.

Rai, S.C. & Bhatia, V.K. (2004): Dimensions of Regional Disparities in Socio-Economic Development of assam, Indian Society of agricultural Statistics, 57 (special volume) New Delhi

CHAPTER 11

The Aromatic Rice's of Assam

Parishmita Hazarika, Nishamani Kar, and Sailajananda Saikia

Abstract

Rice, a staple food crop for half of the world's population, exhibits significant variation in cultivars, particularly in Assam, one of its centres of origin. Aromatic rice represents a small yet significant sub-group of rice, prized for their quality and higher market value compared to non-aromatic varieties. However, improvement efforts for aromatic rice have been slow due to challenges in cross-compatibility with high-yielding non-aromatic varieties, environmental dependencies of quality trait expression, and a lack of comprehensive information.

Assam's aromatic rice varieties, particularly Joha rice, are distinguished by their unique aroma, fine kernel quality, excellent cooking characteristics, and high palatability. Despite their superior qualities, these traditional varieties have not been extensively studied due to various constraints, with only preliminary breeding and tissue culture work conducted locally. The spread of high-yielding varieties during the Green Revolution has further threatened the conservation of these traditional cultivars, many of which are now near extinction.

This review aims to consolidate scattered information on Assam's aromatic rice varieties, particularly Joha rice, to facilitate further research and conservation efforts. Understanding the cultivation, genetic traits, and socio-economic importance of these traditional varieties is crucial for preserving Assam's agricultural biodiversity. Enhanced focus on these varieties can contribute to ecological balance, economic stability, and cultural heritage in the region.

Key words: Aromatic rice, green revolution, diversity, conservation, economic stability.

Introduction

Rice (Oryzasativa L.) was the second most important cereal in the world and it was the staple food for most Asians and over 90% of the world's rice is produced and consumed in Asia. China is the substantial grower, accounting for 30% of the production, followed by India (24%), Bangladesh(7%),

Indonesia (7%), Vietnam (5%), and Thailand (4%). India is also the second-largest consumer of rice (21%) after China. (Bhaduri et al., 2023). India was the second-largest rice-producing country in the world and the crop contributes over 42% to the annual food grain production of the country (Vijayakumar et al., 2021). India is a natural home for rich diversity of rice landraces (Samal et al., 2014). The total production of rice during 2022-23 is estimated at a record 1357.55 lakh tonnes, which is higher by 62.84 lakh tonnes compared to the previous year's production of 1294.71 lakh tonnes and by 153.65 lakh tonnes compared to the average production of the last five years (Ministry of Agriculture & Farmers Welfare, 2023).

Thus, India boasts one of the richest paddy diversities in the world and ranks as the second largest producer of paddy after China. It has the largest area ahead of China under paddy cultivation, spread almost in all the states of the country (Pathak et al., 2018). Located in the northeastern part of India, Assam is one of the leading producers among the top ten rice-producing states in the country. In Assam, rice occupies approximately 70% of the total cropped area, dominating the state's agriculture. Rice, the primary agricultural GDP source, plays a significant role in the state economy (Bordoloi et al., 2024). Assam is a traditionally rice cultivating region where it plays a determinative role in the socio-economy and cultural life of the state. Rice is consumed by about 90 percent of the state population and is grown over an area of 26.46 lakh hectares occupying around 74.25 percent of the cropped area (Basic Agricultural Statistics, 1991-92 to 2019-20).

Assam is considered as one of centres of origin of rice is blessed with greater extent of rich biodiversity comprising of more than 10,000 rice accessions. Rice has vast diversity that might be due to highly variable agro-climatic ecosystems in the state. Thus, large numbers of different traditional rice varieties are grown by the farmers in the state in general including some finest quality aromatic rice in particular (Lahkar, 2018).

Aromatic rice varieties of different shapes and sizes in Assam represent the remarkable genetic diversity found across various agro-climatic regions. Among these, Joha rice holds a unique status due to its excellent quality and long-standing significance in the region. Numerous traditional aromatic rice landraces or cultivars with short grains, exceptional aroma, nutritional properties, and superior cooking qualities are cultivated in different parts of Assam. Farmers grow these rice varieties for both household consumption and sale in domestic markets, where they are highly valued (Lahkar et al., 2017).

However, the influence of the Green Revolution and the increasing demand for higher-yielding rice varieties have led to a decline in the conservation of these traditional varieties, putting many at the brink of extinction (Eliazer et al., 2019). Therefore, it is urgently needed to study about the cultivation and conservation of these unique and valuable rice varieties before they completely disappear from the fields, because the loss of these varieties would not only cause an ecological imbalance in the agricultural biodiversity of the state but also lead to economic and cultural disruptions.

Rice Cultivars of Assam:

Rice is the main life of Assam as it provides both food and nutritional security to more than 3 crore population residing in the state. This crop was grown in a wide diverse condition in Assam. It was grown from deep water area of Dhemaji district to hill slopes of Karbi Anglong. Assam is also bestowed with a rich diversity of rice cultivars, among them are Joha (aromatic), Semi waxy (Chokuwa) waxy (bora), and red bao (Deep and floating) rice which are the unique 'gift of nature'. There are four different types of rice cultivars grown in Assam ie., Ahu (autumn rice) cultivated from March – June month. Sali (winter rice) cultivated from June – Nov/Dec month, Boro (Summer rice) cultivated from Nov- May month. Direct seeded Ahu and Sali rice are grown under rain fed condition having various traits like high starch content, aroma, flavour, waxy, non-waxy, stickiness etc. About 70% of the total agricultural land of Assam is used for rice cultivation (Das et al., 2010).

Evaluation History and Genetic Diversity of Aromatic Rice in Assam:

Rice is one of the oldest staple crops, endowed with great phenomenal genetic resources in Assam. During the course of evolution, rice's genetic resources have diverged into a handful of sub-groups, with specific traits, which are largely cultivated and nurtured by the different ethnic groups in specific regions.

Aromatic, scented, or fragrant rice varieties are a special group that have carved out their niche due to their unique aroma and other cooking quality traits. The first reference to the existence of aromatic rice can be traced to the documents of Susrutha (c. 400 BC), the great Indian pioneer in medicine and surgery (Siddiq et al., 2012; Vemireddy et al., 2020). Assam is widely considered one of the origins of rice and boasts some of the most interesting rice cultivars in India. Aromatic rice contributes to a small group among the cultivated rice in Assam, but acquires a special reference in context to fragrance or aroma. Aroma is one of the main character or quality which affects and defines the popularity of different food products (Saikia et al.,2023).The state has a diverse gene pool of aromatic rice cultivars that differ in intensity of aroma, durability, grain size and shape, yield per hectare, production potential, and other traits.

Therefore, in terms of aroma, longevity, grain size and shape, production ability, and other traits, Assam's aromatic rice, traditionally known as *"joha,"* differs from other aromatic rices. After transplanting seedlings late in the season, *Joha* rice is produced in water adjacent fields, hilly lands, or on Sali seed beds. Joha occupies around 5% of the Sali rice land; with an average yield of 1–1.5 t/ha (Borah et al., 2022).

It appears that Joha rice cultivars have been grown in Assam for centuries. Interestingly, Khorika Joha is mentioned in detail by Kaviraja Madhava Kandali in the 14th-century Assamese version of the Ramayana (Saptakanda Ramayana), which is believed to be one of the earliest written scriptures in the Assamese language. According to this text, Ravana was at his wits' end when all his attempts to rouse his younger brother Kumbha karna from his deep slumber failed. Ravana used every trick he could think of, one of them being to place a heap of delicious food made from Khorika Joha near his nose to tempt his senses (Sahasa, June 1). Thus, from the ancient period of time there are diverse types of aromatic rice have been growing in Assam. Due to which this valuable indigenous rice of Assam also received the Geographical Indication Tag (GI) in 2017. The table1 below showcases the diverse Joha rice cultivars that are meticulously maintained at Assam Agricultural University.

Table 1: Joha Rice Cultivars Maintained at Assam Agricultural University

SL.NO.	CULTIVAR	SL.NO.	CULTIVAR	SL.NO.	CULTIVAR
1	Ahu joha	19	Goalporia joha 1	34	kon joha3
2	Arab joha	20	Goalporia joha 2	35	Kotari bhog
3	Baberi joha	21	Gobind bhog	36	Krisha joha
4	Badshah bhog	22	Joha	37	Kunkuni joha
5	Bakul joha	23	Joha bora	38	Maniki madhuri
6	Bengali joha	24	Kamini joha	39	Nepali joha
7	Bhaboli joha	25	Gobindatulsi joha	40	Rampal joha
8	Bhugi joha	26	kala jeera	41	Ranga joha1
9	Bhugri joha	27	Guti joha	42	Ranga joha2
10	Boga joha	25	Kal gira	43	Tulsi bhog
11	Bogi joha	26	Kapow Salijoha	44	Tulsi joha
12	Bogamani kimadhuri	27	Khori kajoha	45	Mukuta joha
13	Bogatulsi joha	28	Kola joha1	46	Kola kunkuni joha
14	Bor joha	29	Kola joha2	47	Bogakunkuni Joha
15	Borsali	30	Koli joha	48	Dangor joha

16	Cheniguti joha	31	Konbogi joha	49	Gufur phisajwsa
17	Chubon joha	32	Kon joha1	50	Betguti joha
18	Chufop joha	33	Kon joha2		

Source: Sarma et al., 2003

IMPORTANCE OF AROMATIC RICE:

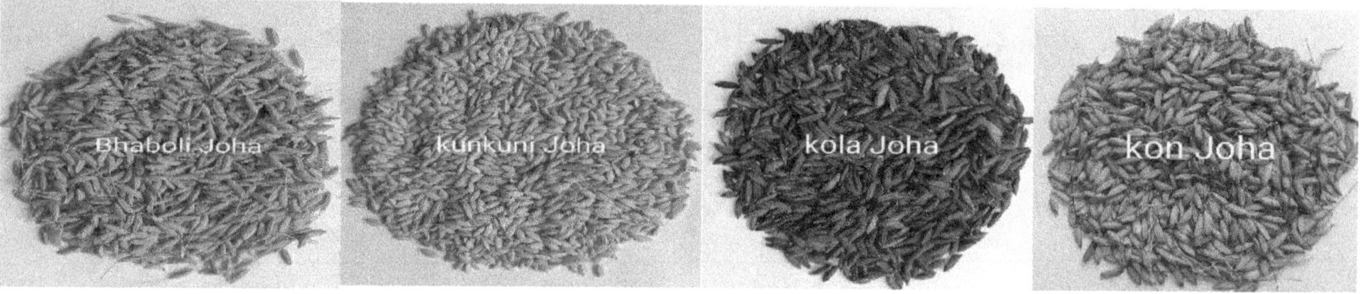

Traditional aromatic rice varieties were developed by natural process locally under the evolutionary force by means of natural selection. These varieties were very unique with their identity and mostly traditional varieties having their importance due to their trait and its economic importance like, protein rice, aroma, unique taste, protein rich, iron, zinc, vitamins, melaic acid, antioxidant rich or more metabolic or molecular activity with medicinal values etc (Ghosh et al., 2022).

On the other hand, traditional varieties were the source of different biotic and abiotic stress tolerance source due to which some time traditional varieties performed batter in adverse condition and preferably cultivated by the farmers in the respective region or spots or so called as hotspot. Sinha and Mishra, (2014) also reported the important of these rice diversity in the sustainable development (Ghosh et al., 2022).

➢ **Nutritional Values of Aromatic Rice of Assam:**

Different types of rice are to grown in Assam among them aromatic rice is highly valued and demands for special attention. The rice is indeed a special heirloom grain of Assam, known for its superfine kernel, sweet scented aroma, good cooking qualities and excellent taste. The unique taste and aroma of the rice is mostly due to the presence of a chemical compound 2-acetyl 1-pyroline which is responsible for their fragrant aroma and taste (Kumar, 2021).

Joha rice is an intermediate of typical Indica and Japonica class. It belongs to medium slender or medium broad category with an L: B (length: breadth ratio) less than 3(Das et al.,2010).According to one of the study done by Sarma and Pathak (1990, 1997) observed that there are high coefficient of variation for 1000-grain weight, yield/plant, panicle weight and EBT/ plant among the Joha varieties, with low variability for hulling and milling percentage, but high variation for head rice recovery, kernel length, breadth, L/B ratio, elongation and alkali value making it a commercially more promising trait then the other varieties of rice. The following table 2 compares the physical properties of Joha rice cultivars to those of Basmati rice:

Table 2: Physical quality characters of Joharice

CHARACTERS	JOHA CULTIVARS	BASMATI
Type	Short-medium grained	Long slender grained
Length- breadth ratio	Less than 3	More than 3
Elongation after cooking	1.4 Times, but breaks	1.8 times without breaking
Aroma	Strong	Strong
Yield potential	Low	High

Source: Das et al., 2010

Another study conducted by Ahmed et al. (1995, 1998) involved a chemical analysis of seven local Joha rice varieties, comparing them with two improved varieties, Basmati and Kasturi. The study found that Joha rice has a crude protein content ranging from 9.17% to 11.67%, which is comparable to that of Basmati and Kasturi. Variations in protein, amylase, amylopectin, and mineral contents were attributed to genetic makeup and environmental influences.

Notably, Joha rice varieties exhibited higher levels of albumin, globulin, and amylase, iron, calcium, phosphorus. These components are essential for protein digestibility and biological value. The typical albumin: globulin: prolamin ratio in Joha rice cultivars from Assam is 11:1:6:70. This ratio highlights the significant nutritional profile of Joha rice, positioning it as a nutritionally rich alternative to Basmati and Kasturi.

Table 3: Range, Mean of Chemical Composition of Joha Cultivars as Compared to basmati and Kasturi

CHEMICAL COMPOSITION	RANGE	MEAN ± SE	BASMATI	KASTURI
Grain crude protein(%N× 5.95)	9.17-11.67	10.72± 0.062	9.69	11.77
Soluble protein (%)	4.62-6.48	5.56 ±0.016	5.04	6.21
Protein fractions (% of				

extracted protein)				
Albumin	11.84-15.12	13.00 ± 0.064	14.37	12.12
Globulin	13.60-18.12	15.00 ± 0.061	15.75	13.04
Prolamine	5.34-6.20	6.00 ± 0.058	5.12	5.54
Glutelin	61.00-68.30	66.00 ± 0.070	64.75	69.00
Total soluble sugar (%)	0.425-0.863	0.522 ± 0.004	0.725	0.425
Reducing sugar (%)	0.125-0.154	0.137 ± 0.003	0.104	0.144
Non – reducing sugar (%)	0.298-0.714	0.433 ± 0.005	0.585	0.281
Starch (%)	67.50-77.85	74.56 ± 0.569	72.00	77.00
Amylose (%)	19.58-23.20	21.06 ± 0.033	20.53	18.90
Amylopectin (%)	76.80-80.42	78.94 ± 0.032	79.47	81.10
Phosphorus(%)	0.210-0.355	0.294± 0.028	0.279	0.270
Calcium (%)	0.017-0.026	0.021 ± 0.005	0.019	0.019
Iron (mg/100g)	1.5- 5.0	3.2 ± 0.001	3.2	2.3

Source: Ahmed et al., 1995, 1998.

> ➢ **Medicinal values of aromatic rice of Assam:**

Joha rice, known as aromatic rice from Assam, is valued not only for its unique flavour but also for its medicinal properties. Scientists at the Institute of Advanced Study in Science and Technology (IASST), an autonomous institute of the Department of Science and Technology explored the nutraceutical properties of aromatic Joha rice. Raj lakshmi Devi along with Paramita Choudhury in their research explored the nutraceutical properties of aromatic Joha rice. Through *in vitro* laboratory analysis, they detected two unsaturated fatty acids viz., linoleic acid (omega-6) and linolenic (omega-3) acid. These essential fatty acids (which human cannot produce) can help maintain various physiological conditions. Omega-3 fatty acid prevents several metabolic diseases such as diabetes, cardiovascular diseases, and cancer. Joha has also proved to be effective in lowering the blood glucose and preventing diabetes onset in diabetic rats.

The researchers also found that scented Joha rice has a more balanced ratio of omega-6 to omega-3 in comparison to the widely consumed non-scented variety. The ratio of omega-6 to omega-3 essential fatty acids (EFA) of required by human beings for maintaining the proper diet is around one. They have used this Joha rice to make rice bran oil, a patented product that they claim to be effective in diabetes management.

Besides, Joha rice is also rich in several antioxidants, flavonoids, and phenolics. Some of the reported bioactive compounds are oryzanol, ferulic acid, tocotrienol, caffeic acid, catechuic acid, gallic acid, tricin, and so on, each with reported antioxidant, hypoglycaemic and cardio-protective effects(Ministry of Science & Technology,23 June, 2023;Rahman et al., 2015;Lahkar et al 2020).

➢ **Socio- economic values of aromatic rice of Assam:**

As an agrarian state, Assam's rice diversity is intricately linked not only to its economy but also to the rich cultural heritage of the region. Assam is endowed with almost more than 40 well linked cultural and natural aromatic rice diversities formed by various ethnic groups, and each group having its own cultures, festivals and rituals. Rice forms an integral part of all social and religious ceremonies and no festivals or rituals are complete without preparations of rice (Sarma et al., 2003).

In culinary traditions, aromatic rice varieties like Kon Joha, Kola Joha are celebrated for their unique flavours and fragrances, enhancing traditional dishes like "Pulao" and "Kheer". Even in everyday meals, these rice varieties are preferred for their superior taste and texture, with simple preparations like steamed Joha rice served with fish curry or dal being common in Assamese households. The religious significance of aromatic rice is also profound. It is often used in religious offerings in temples across Assam due to its purity and quality, making it a preferred choice for prasadam (sacred food). During important Hindu rituals, aromatic rice is utilized in various forms, including cooked rice, sweets, and ceremonial offerings (Naivedya), underscoring its integral role in Assamese spiritual practices.

Aroma is a major characteristic of rice quality that increases the potential value of rice in the international trade. Over the past half-century, the demand of aromatic rice for special purpose has dramatically increased (Verma et al., 2018). Aromatic varieties fetch higher price in rice market than the non-aromatic ones. Aromatic rice varieties in Assam, particularly Joha rice, play a crucial role in the state's economy by driving agricultural revenue, creating employment, and boosting trade. These rice varieties are in high demand both domestically and internationally due to their unique flavour and aroma, fetching premium prices that enhance farmers' incomes. With substantial export potential and geographical indication (GI) status, Joha rice enjoys strong brand recognition in global markets (Lakra et al.,2014).In the following table, it can be seen that in the local markets, among all the rice varieties, Joha rice fetches a higher market value (65 Rs/kg) than others.

Table 4: Prevailing market prices of dehulled rice in local market of Assam (March, 2024).

CLASSES OF DEHULLED RICE	EXAMPLE	MARKET PRICE (RS/KG)	USES
Medium slender	Mahsuri	40-45	Consumption
Medium bold	Pankaj	40-45	Consumption
Bora rice(glutinous rice)	Ghew bora	45-50	Traditional cakes,

			breakfast and beverages
Chakowa rice(semi glutinous soft rice)	Nepali chakowa	50-55	Breakfast, instant rice
Joha rice (medium, short bold or fine grained, aromatic)	Kola joha	60-65	Consumption(occasional), kheer, polao etc.

Environmental Influence on Aromatic Rice Cultivation in Assam:

Aroma development in rice is governed by both genetic as well as environmental factors (Lahkar, 2018). Weather parameters play a key role in quality determination of aromatic rice. Rice requires warm and humid climate during vegetative period and relatively cooler temperature at grain filling stage for optimum growth, yield, and quality (singh et al., 2019).Assam is one the seven states of northeast India, which is located between 22°19′ to 28°16′North Latitude and 89°42′ to 96°30′ East Longitude. Assam is situated in the North-East of India and is the largest north eastern state in terms of population while second in terms of area. Assam covers an area of 78,438 km2 (30,285 sq miles). The state is bordered by Bhutan and the state of Arunachal Pradesh to the north; Nagaland, Arunachal Pradesh and Manipur to the east; Meghalaya, Tripura, Mizoram, and Bangladesh to the south; and West Bengal to the west. A significant geographical aspect of Assam is that it contains three of six physiographic divisions of India – The Northern Himalayas (Eastern Hills), The Northern Plains (Brahmaputra plain), and the Deccan Plateau (Karbi Anglong).

The Barak and the Brahmaputra rivers with their innumerable tributaries are the sources of water for Assam. These rivers supply water for growing different crops in the state. The climate of Assam is typically 'Tropical Monsoon Rainforest Climate', with high levels of humidity and heavy rainfall. People here enjoy a moderate climate all throughout the year, with warm summers and mild winters (summer max. at 95-100 °F or 35-38 °C and winter min. at 43-46 °F or 6-8 °C). Spring (March–April) and autumn (September–October) are usually pleasant with moderate rainfall and temperature. Assam's agriculture usually depends on the south-west monsoon rains (https://cm.assam.gov.in/state-profile).

The state's unique climatic and physiographic features are highly favourable for rice cultivation, allowing the crop to be grown in a wide range of agro-ecological conditions. Rice is cultivated from hill slopes to deep-water areas, during both the wet humid months and the drier periods of the year. These variations in physiographic features and climatic conditions have resulted in three distinct rice growing seasons: Autumn (February/March – June/July), winter (June/July – November/December), and summer (November/December – May/June). To adapt to these diverse land situations and varying growing seasons, a wide variety of rice has been traditionally grown in the state since ancient times, ensuring agricultural resilience and abundance in the state.

Conservation Efforts:

Efforts to conserve aromatic rice varieties in Assam involve both in-situ and ex-situ strategies. In-situ conservation includes maintaining traditional farming systems and supporting local seed banks, while ex-situ methods involve the preservation of genetic material in seed vaults and research institutions. Organizations such as the Assam Agricultural University and various NGOs are actively engaged in these conservation efforts.

➤ **Ex-situ conservation:**

Local farmers in Assam have traditionally cultivated rice varieties based on their knowledge of quality and adaptation to various agro-ecological systems. However, during the latter half of the 20th century, the push for intensive agriculture to increase crop yields and meet the growing demand for food has led to the degradation of essential natural resources such as soil, water, and natural genetic diversity. In recent decades, biotechnological solutions to enhance food production have surged, motivating farmers to adopt hybrid and high-yielding varieties at the expense of traditional ones. Researchers have highlighted the importance of in situ conservation as a complementary approach to ex situ conservation to address genetic erosion (Talukdar et al., 2017).

The Agricultural University of Assam plays a crucial role in the ex-situ conservation of rice in the state. Extensive research conducted by the university focuses on preserving the genetic diversity of rice. Various rice research institutions under Assam Agricultural University (AAU), such as the Assam Rice Research Institute (ARRI) in Titabar and the Zonal Research Stations in Karimganj and North Lakhimpur, are actively studying, collecting, and conserving different traditional rice varieties across the state.

According to a study by Saikia et al. (2023), a total of 377 traditional paddy varieties have been collected from across the state by the AAU-Zonal Research Station in North Lakhimpur, which currently maintains this collection. This includes 146 varieties of Sali rice and 231 varieties of deep-water rice (Bao) germplasm. Similarly, AAU-ARRI in Titabar has been preserving 7,000 accessions of various indigenous rice cultivars, indicating a strong focus on ex situ conservation of rice varieties.

The government of Assam also places significant emphasis on conserving rice biodiversity. The Assam State Biodiversity Board (ASBB) and the Department of Agriculture, Assam, are actively working to conserve and promote the cultivation of traditional rice varieties. They conduct various workshops and programs to motivate farmers to continue growing these traditional varieties.

> ➢ **In- Situ conservation:**

To support the cultivation of traditional rice varieties, the government has implemented various schemes and policies, such as the Protection of Plant Varieties and Farmers' Rights Act, 2001 (PPVFR Act) and the Geographical Indications of Goods (Registration and Protection) Act, 1999 (GIs Act). These initiatives have encouraged traditional rice farmers to continue cultivating and conserving their valuable rice varieties by providing official recognition.

Table: List farmers awarded the Plant Genome Saviour Award.

YEAR	SR. NO.	FARMER NAME
2012	1	Manik Saikia
2012	2	Jitul Saikia
2012	3	Suren Saikia
2016-17	4	Prabin Saikia
2016-17	5	Mohan Chandra Borah
2023-24	6	Suren Saikia

Source: Ministry of Agriculture and Farmers Welfare, Government of India.

As of now, more than five farmers from Assam have been awarded the Plant Genome Saviour Award under the Protection of Plant Varieties and Farmers' Rights Authority (PPVFRA) in collaboration with the Department of Agriculture and Cooperation, Ministry of Agriculture and Farmers Welfare, Government of India, for their in-situ conservation of plant varieties. Among them, Mr. Manik Saikia, Mr. Suren Bora has been mainly recognized for theirin-situ conservation of numerous Deep Water Sali and Ahu rice varieties since they began their agricultural endeavours.

Additionally, another farmer from the Jorhat district of Assam, Mr. Mohan Chandra Borah, has been recognized for his contribution by establishing a seed conservation library called "Annapurna," which houses more than 500 varieties of rice (Indian Express, 7th January 2024). To protect and preserve local varieties of rice from extinction due to the widespread use of high-yielding seeds, a young farmer, Mr Dwipen Baruah, in the Bhogamukh area, has also collected 60 local varieties from paddy fields in Sivasagar and Jorhat districts (The Assam Tribune on 15th September 2010). Additionally, the

Assam State Biodiversity Strategy and Action Plan (2017-2030) is taking initiatives to motivate farmers to continue cultivating their traditional genetic rice diversities.

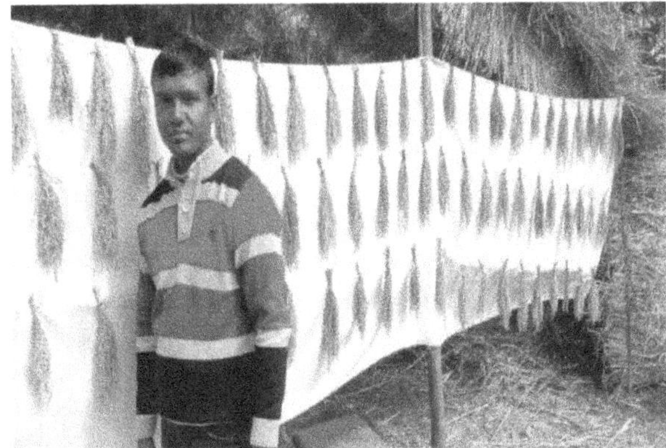

Figure 1: Plant Genome Savior Award received by Mr Suren Bora; Figure 2: Mr Mohan Chandra Borah (Annapurna seed Library founder of Assam).

Challenges to Conservation:

Non availability of quality seeds, low productivity, severe attack of pest and diseases, and low price of produce are identified as the major constraints in aromatic rice production. Market constraints and restrictions result in erosion in diversity of aromatic rice. The quality of aromatic rice is the most important aspect valued by the consumers in domestic and international market. In spite of high market price and export potential, the area expansion and adoption by the farmers have not reached to the desired extent. Various productions, managerial, technological, and socioeconomic issues are associated with low adoption. Such problems vary within and between the rice-growing ecologies (Singh et al., 2019) listed below:

> **Genetic Erosion**:

The allure of high-yielding, hybrid rice varieties is leading farmers to abandon their time-tested traditional strains. This shift erodes the rich genetic diversity of rice in Assam, which is essential for crop resilience and long-term agricultural sustainability in the face of unforeseen challenges in the state.

> **Climate Change:**

Climate change is resulting in erratic weather patterns, including unpredictable monsoons, floods, and droughts. These changes disrupt traditional farming practices and make it challenging for the farmers to maintain the cultivation of traditional rice varieties that are often adapted to specific local conditions.

➢ **Market Pressures**:

Although there is a higher market demand and better prices for traditional rice varieties, these prices fluctuate due to seasonal demand variations, making them more accessible to the financially well-off rather than the local population. This economic pressure forces farmers to prioritize crops that offer immediate financial returns, leading to a decline in the cultivation of these traditional rice varieties.

➢ **Middleman Intervention**:

Middleman intervention is one of the major problems in Assam. The presence of middlemen in the supply chain often reduces the profit margins for farmers. Middlemen typically purchase rice at lower prices from farmers and sell it at higher rates in the market, discouraging farmers from cultivating traditional varieties that might not yield immediate financial benefits.

➢ **Land holding Size**:

In every passing year with the increasing size of population the land holding size of farmers are decreasing in Assam. Thus, many farmers in Assam have small plots of land, which limits their ability to grow diverse traditional rice varieties. Apart from that with such small landholdings, the farmers now a day's mainly try to focus on maximizing yield, often choosing high-yield crops over traditional varieties to make the most of their limited space.

➢ **Lack of Awareness**:

Although many farmers are being recognized and benefited for their conservation work, many others remain unaware of the various schemes and benefits provided by the government to them. This lack of awareness hinders the preservation of traditional rice varieties. There is insufficient dissemination of information regarding the benefits of traditional rice, including its nutritional value, cultural significance, and environmental adaptability.

➢ **Pest and Disease Pressure**:

With changing climatic patterns, traditional rice varieties have become more vulnerable to pests and diseases due to the lack of modern agricultural practices. Limited research and development focused on protecting these varieties from biotic stress further threaten their conservation in the state.

➤ **Infrastructure Challenges**:

Traditional rice varieties in the state face a double threat due to infrastructure challenges. Poor storage facilities on farms lead to substantial post-harvest losses, while limited market access makes it difficult for farmers to sell their rice. This combination reduces profitability and discourages cultivation, threatening both the livelihoods of farmers and the state's unique rice biodiversity.

➤ **Policy Gaps**:

While there are policies supporting traditional rice conservation, but their implementation and enforcement are often inadequate. Comprehensive policies that address the specific needs and challenges faced by traditional rice farmers are lacking, leading to insufficient support for conservation efforts of these valuable varieties of rice.

➤ **Resource Limitations**:

Farmers often face financial and technical constraints in the state that often hinder their ability to conserve traditional varieties. There is also lack of access to modern conservation technologies, infrastructure, and financial support, making it difficult for farmers to maintain traditional cultivation practices in the state.

Addressing these multifaceted challenges requires a holistic approach, encompassing policy reforms, increased awareness, improved infrastructure, and targeted support to ensure the preservation and sustainable cultivation of Assam's traditional rice varieties.

Future Prospects of Aromatic Rice:

Aromatic rice varieties from Assam, such as Joha, hold a special place in both domestic and international markets due to their exceptional quality and unique aroma, commanding prices almost three times higher than non-aromatic varieties. The demand for Assam's aromatic rice is steadily increasing every year, reaching various parts of the world. However, the export market share for several unique short-grain aromatic varieties from Assam remains minimal. To enhance the global presence and ensure the sustainability of these varieties, a focus on conservation and improved cultivation practices is essential. Conservation strategies must be prioritized to preserve the rich genetic diversity of Assam's aromatic rice. In situ conservation, where farmers continue to cultivate traditional varieties in their natural habitats, maintains genetic diversity and traditional farming practices. Organizations like the Assam Agricultural University and various rice research stations are actively involved in collecting, studying, and preserving different rice germ plasms. Educating farmers about the benefits of conserving traditional rice varieties, including their nutritional value, cultural significance, and environmental adaptability, is vital.

Improving cultivation practices is another key aspect of ensuring the future of Assam's aromatic rice. Given the unique climatic and physiographic conditions of Assam, tailored agricultural practices that enhance yield while maintaining quality are necessary. Sustainable farming techniques, such as organic farming and integrated pest management, can help mitigate the vulnerability of traditional varieties to pests and diseases.

Additionally, improving infrastructure for better storage and market access will reduce post-harvest losses and increase profitability for farmers. Establishing direct market links and reducing middlemen intervention can ensure farmers receive fair prices for their produce. Encouraging value addition, such as packaging and branding of aromatic rice, can further enhance marketability and consumer appeal. The future prospects of aromatic rice in Assam hinge on a balanced approach that includes effective conservation strategies, improved cultivation practices, economic empowerment of farmers, and targeted research and development.

Conclusion:

Aromatic rice is specialty rice of global repute with distinct quality standards. These varieties have been grown in Assam for centuries, playing a significant role in the state's economy and farmers' livelihoods. Traditionally cultivated, aromatic rice are long-duration crops and less responsive to applied inputs (Singh et al., 2019). The introduction of high-yielding and better-quality varieties has shifted the research focus from aromatic to modern non-aromatic rice varieties, leading to subsistence farming of aromatic varieties.

The decrease in area under the cultivation of aromatic rice in addition to low productivity, pest susceptibility and unavailability of quality seeds as a result of increasing erosion of genetic diversity discourage farmers from cultivation of aromatic rice. Economic constraints such as limited financial support from financial institutions, lack of better infrastructure and transportation facilities for processed rice are faced by the farmers. Erosion of aromatic rice diversity is a huge problem which is mainly due to small farm sizes as a result of which farmers are able to cultivate only a small quantity of a particular aromatic rice variety. Inability of the farmers to retain the produce for seeds further contributes to the continuous disappearance of aromatic rice varieties. Due to the non-replacement of seeds for years together, seed quality gets deteriorated due to which several valuable aromatic rice varieties in the past 20 years have either become extinct or are on the verge of extinction. Protection of high-value aromatic genotypes requires active participation of farmers (Dutta et al., 2019).

Therefore, there is an urgent need to document, evaluate, conserve and utilize the underutilized germ plasm of aromatic rice of Assam, because preserving these rice varieties is not only crucial for maintaining biodiversity but also for sustaining the cultural heritage and livelihoods of local communities. Continued efforts in research, conservation, and sustainable agriculture are essential to ensure the survival of these unique rice varieties for future generations.

References:

Ahmed, S.A. 1993. Studies on the chemical Composition of some rice varieties grown in Assam. M.Sc. (Agri) Thesis, Assam Agril. University, Jorhat.

Ahmed, S.A., Barua, I. and Das, D. 1998. Chemical Composition of scented rice. Oryza. 32: 167-169.

Ahmed, S.A., Barua, I. and Pathak, A.k. 1999. Market Potential of Joha rice in Assam. In Abs: 4th Agricultural Science Congress, 21-24 feb, 1999, Jaipur: 66.

Bhaduri, D., Vijayakumar, S., Daripa, A., Verma, B. C., &Mohanty, S. (2023). Carbon Footprint in Rice Cultivation. In *Handbook of Energy Management in Agriculture* (pp. 3-38). Singapore: Springer Nature Singapore.

Blakeney, M., Krishnankutty, J., Raju, R. K., & Siddique, K. H. (2020). Agricultural innovation and the protection of traditional rice varieties: Kerala a case study. *Frontiers in sustainable food systems, 3*, 116.

Borah, N., Sarma, R. N., Borah, V. V., &Behera, P. P. (2022). Status of genomic research in non-basmati aromatic Joha rice of Assam. *International Journal of Environment and Climate Change, 12*(10), 338-347.

Bordoloi, D., Sarma, D., SarmaBarua, N., Das, R., & Das, B. K. (2024). Morpho-molecular and nutritional profiling for yield improvement and value addition of indigenous aromatic Joha rice of Assam. *Scientific Reports, 14*(1), 3509.

Chetia, S. K., Hazarika, G., Bordoloi, S., Talukdar, M., Tamuly, A., Das, B. C., ... & Ahmed, T. (2019). Screening of traditional scented rice (Johä) of Assam for presence of Badh2, blast and brown spot diseases. *ORYZA-An International Journal on Rice, 56*(2), 204-208.

Das, A., Kesari, V., &Rangan, L. (2010). Aromatic joha rice of Assam-A review. *Agricultural Reviews, 31*(1), 1-10.

Dias, L. G., Hacke, A., dos Santos Souza, E., Nath, S., Canesin, M. R., Vilella, O. V., ... &Bragagnolo, N. (2022). Comparison of chemical and nutritional compositions between aromatic and non-aromatic rice from Brazil and effect of planting time on bioactive compounds. *Journal of Food Composition and Analysis*, *111*, 104608.

Dutta, C., Nath, D. J., &Phyllei, D. (2022). Aromatic rice and factors affecting aroma in rice. *Int. J. Environ. Climate Change*, *12*(11), 1773-1779.

Eliazer Nelson, A. R. L., Ravichandran, K., & Antony, U. (2019). The impact of the Green Revolution on indigenous crops of India. *Journal of Ethnic Foods*, *6*(1), 1-10.

Ghosh, S. C., Manika, N., Gupta, S., Singh, M., Dasgupta, T., &Khanuja, S. P. S. (2022). Future Prospective: Traditional Rice (Oryzasativa L.) of Eastern India. International Journal of Advanced Research, 10(10), 770-779.

Habibur Rahman, H. R., Eswaraiah, M. C., & Dutta, A. M. (2015). In-vitro anti-inflammatory and anti-arthritic activity of Oryzasativa var. Joha rice (an aromatic indigenous rice of Assam).

https://cm.assam.gov.in/state-profile

https://plantauthority.gov.in/details-plant-genome-saviour-farmer-honor-winners

Iqbal, A. (2023). See discussions, stats, and author profiles for this publication at: https://www. researchgate. net/publication/323614212 Ovarian Leiomyoma Associated with Serous Cystadenoma-A Case Report of an Uncommon Entity Ovarian Leiomyoma Associated with Serous Cystadenoma-A Case Report of an Uncommon Entity.

Kowsalya, P., Sharanyakanth, P. S., &Mahendran, R. (2022). Traditional rice varieties: A comprehensive review on its nutritional, medicinal, therapeutic and health benefit potential. *Journal of Food Composition and Analysis*, *114*, 104742.

Kumar, B. M. (2021). *Evaluation of aromatic rice genotypes against blast and its biointensive management under rainfed condition* (Doctoral thesis, Assam Agricultural University). http://hdl.handle.net/10603/490265

Lahkar, L. (2018). Morphological, biochemical, and molecular characterization of traditional aromatic rice landraces of Assam (Doctoral thesis). Gauhati University.

Lahkar, L., Hazarika, G., & Tanti, B. (2020). Proximate composition, physicochemical and antioxidant properties revealed the potentiality of traditional aromatic (Joha) rice as functional food. *Vegetos*, *33*, 40-51.

Lakra, A. K., Sh, C., Ch, S. F., Pratap, B., &Lakra, P. (2014). To study the economic importance of rice (Oryzasativa L.) varieties suitable for organic farming. *Journal of Plant Development Sciences*, *6*(1), 105-107.

Mackill, D. J., Ismail, A. M., Pamplona, A. M., Sanchez, D. L., Carandang, J. J., &Septiningsih, E. M. (2010). Stress tolerant rice varieties for adaptation to a changing climate. *Crop, Environment & Bioinformatics*, *7*, 250-259.

Ministry of Agriculture & Farmers Welfare. (2023, October 18). Final estimates of production of major crops released for the year 2022-23. Retrieved from https://pib.gov.in/newsite/pmreleases.aspx?mincode=27

Ministry of Science & Technology. (2023, June 23). Joha rice -- the nutraceutical of choice in diabetes management. *Press Information Bureau Delhi*. Retrieved from https://www.pib.gov.in/PressReleasePage.aspx?PRID=1934733 .

Rahaman, H., Eswaraiah, M. C., & Dutta, A. M. (2015). Joha Rice: An aromatic indigenous rice of Assam, India contains flavanoids and phenolic substances and shows good antioxidant activities. *Der Pharmacia Lettre*, *7*, 212-217.

Sahasa. (2021, June 1). Joha rice of Assam. *Sahasa*. Retrieved from https://sahasa.in/2021/06/01/joha-rice-of-assam/

Saikia, P., Chowdhury, D., Gogoi, N. K., Das, Y., &Ozah, B. (2023). Biodiversity at AAU-Zonal Research Station, North Lakhimpur: Green Audit -A technical booklet published by the Chief Scientist, AAU-Zonal Research Station, North Lakhimpur, pp 1-33.

Saikia, P., Neog, B., Borgohain, B., Baruah, D., Gogoi, N., Borthakur, A., &Gogoi, A. (2023). Quantification of 2-acetyl-1-pyrroline in Joha rice and its correlation with agromorphological characters with special reference to upper Brahmaputra valley, Assam, India. *Flora and Fauna, 29*(1), 3-10.

Sharma, N. K., Sharma, K. K., Hazarika, G. N., Saikia, L., & Singh, R. K. (2003). The aromatic rices of Assam. In R. K. Singh & U. S. Singh (Eds.), A treatise on the scented rices of India (pp. 231-249*). Kalyani Publishers.*

Singh, S. P., Singh, M. K., Kumar, S., &Sravan, U. S. (2019). Cultivation of aromatic rice: A review. *Agronomic Crops: Volume 1: Production Technologies*, 175-198.

Statistical Handbook of Assam. (1991-91 to 2019-20). Directorate of Economics and Statistics, Government of Assam.

Sunita, O. K. K. (2022). Evaluation of aromatic rice of India. *World Journal of Pharmacy and Pharmaceutical Sciences, 11*(10), 103-113.

Talukdar, N. R., & Choudhury, P. (2017). Factors associated with agrobiodiversity conservation: A case study on conservation of rice varieties in Barak valley, Assam, India. *Journal of Scientific Agriculture, 1*, 79-90.

The Assam Tribune. (2010, September 15). Farmer collects 60 varieties of local rice. Retrieved from https://assamtribune.com/farmer-collects-60-varieties-of-local-rice

The Indian Express. (2024, January 7). Assam's Mahan Chandra Borah pays tribute to rice. Retrieved from https://www.newindianexpress.com/good-news/2024/Jan/07/assams-mahan-chandra-borah-paystribute-to-rice-2648632.html

Vemireddy, L. R., Tanti, B., Lahkar, L., &Shandilya, Z. M. (2021). Aromatic rices: Evolution, genetics and improvement through conventional breeding and biotechnological methods. *Molecular Breeding for Rice Abiotic Stress Tolerance and Nutritional Quality*, 341-357.

Verma, D. K., Srivastav, P. P., &Nadaf, A. (2018). Aromatic rice from different countries: an overview. *SCIENCE and TECHNOLOGY of Aroma, Flavour and Fragrance in Rice*, 93-140.

Vijayakumar, S., Dinesh, Kumar, Dinesh, Jinger., Bhargavi, Bussa., Panda, B.B., 2021. 4R nutrient stewardship based potassium fertilization for dry-direct seeded rice-wheat cropping system. Indian Farming 71(01), 22–25.

Wang, R., Rejesus, R. M., Tack, J. B., Balagtas, J. V., & Nelson, A. D. (2022). Quantifying the yield sensitivity of modern rice varieties to warming temperatures: Evidence from the philippines. *American Journal of Agricultural Economics, 104*(1), 318-339.

CHAPTER 12

River Bank Instability Analysis in Borgang River, Biswanath District, Assam

---

Latifa Ara Khanam and Santanu Kumar Patnaik

Abstract

In a developing country like India, the rapid and ever-increasing population has exerted a lot of pressure on the natural resources thereby changing the land use and land cover pattern. River bank erosion is a common and natural phenomenon in the world determining the changes in the channel of a river. The river bank instability mapping analysis plays an important role in determining the erosion and deposition affected areas. To understand the spatio-temporal changes of the river, the present study focused on the river bank instability analysis in Borgang River of Biswanath district. The satellite images for the year 2003 and 2023 were used and extracted and further processed under GIS environment. During the period of 20 years (2003-2023), the river has eroded about 5.31 km of bankline areas. This reveals that the river has high erosivity index and is highly instable causing tremendous changes in its channel pattern thereby directly affecting the settlement. The Remote Sensing technology has helped a lot in order to identify the instability changes with reference to spatio-temporal analysis. Keeping this in mind, the concerned government must take certain initiatives for better planning and development providing some basic amenities to the homeless people.

Key Words: River bank, Geospatial tools, Borgang River

Introduction

Erosion, transportation and deposition are the key elements of a river. River bank erosion, a natural phenomena can be defined as the wearing down away of the banks of a stream or river. When the river overflows its banks, it creates natural calamities (Baishya, 2013). It is a very common phenomenon in the middle and lower course of the rivers. It is a very dynamic process occurring rapidly for a short residence resulting in the river meandering and bank instability. Bank erosion is a combination of inter-related factors like flow characteristics, composition of bank materials, sediment deposits and channel geometry. The bank materials in the Brahmaputra River are highly susceptible to erosion due to the presence of high moisture content, low clay content and very poor graded of fine and silt. The braided nature of the river consists of large meanders, variable number of channels, sandbars are temporary in nature.

The Brahmaputra River is one of the braided rivers consisting of numerous channels. Due to flattening of the river gradient, the river becomes much braided in nature. Borgang River, one of the tributaries of Brahmaputra have very steep slope up to a considerable distance carrying heavy boulders and heavy silt charge. This causes heavy flooding in the lower part of the river and abrupt modifications in the flow pattern. Anthropogenic activities along the river side includes deforestation, construction of bridges and dams, artificial cut offs and land use changes bring disequilibrium in the river dynamics accelerating the rate of bank erosion (Das and et al, 2014).

Borgang River is situated in the north part of Biswanath district facing the problem of acute erosion. The river is continuously shifting its course widening its channel causing loss of land cover, loss of settlements. The problem also identifies that the water level of the river in the district has been increasing due to incessant rains from the past years. With this impact, a large number of paddy fields, small tea gardens have been surged under the water of the river. Therefore, the present paper attempts to study the river bank instability analysis of Borgang River in Biswanath district at 1:50,000 scale in GIS environment in order to identify the potential zones of erosion.

Study area

Biswanath district is located between the mighty River Brahmaputra and the Himalayan foothills of Arunachal Pradesh. It extends between 92° 16′ E to 93° 43′ E longitudes and 26° 30′ N to 27° 01′ N latitudes bounded by Arunachal Pradesh in its north, River Brahmaputra in its south, Sonitpur district in its west and North Lakhimpur in its east. The total geographical area of the district is about 1796 square kilometers (Statistical Handbook Assam, 2021). The district comprises four revenue circles – Naduar, Biswanath, Helem and Gohpur. The number of rivers originating in the Himalayan foothills flows southwards and ultimately confluence with Brahmaputra creating an alluvial fertile plain in the district. Ghiladhari, Burhigang, Borgang, Behali comes under Biswanath sub-division while Burhoi, Solengi, Kharoi, Balijan, Mornoi comes under Gohpur sub-division. Borgang River, a tributary of the

Brahmaputra originates from Daphla hills of Arunachal Pradesh. It flows through Daphla hills and Noamara and Dikal are the two tributaries of Borgang before its confluence with Brahmaputra.

Physiographically, the district is plain and the River Brahmaputra forms the southern boundary of the district dotted with many beels and marshy areas.   As per 2011 census, the population is about 6,12,491 of which 31,368 live in urban areas. The district has a population density of about 560 sq km with sex ratio of 968 females per 1000 males. Being a part of the Brahmaputra valley, the district enjoys sub-tropical and monsoon type of climate. Summers are hot and humid with an average temperature of 29° C. The climatic characteristics of the district are highly seasonal rainfall in the form of heavy showers leading to inundation, river bank erosion during and post flood occurrence.

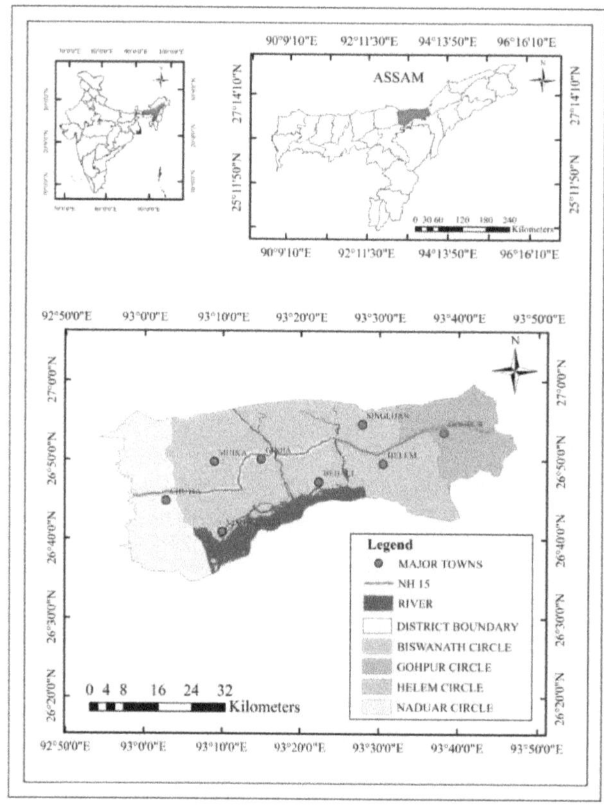

Source: Prepared by Author
Figure 1. Location map of the study area

Objectives

The major objective of the study:

a.   To analyze the river bank instability of Borgang river during 2003 and 2023.

Database and methodology

The present study is based on secondary data. The study of bank instability of Borgang River in Biswanath district is carried out with GIS techniques. The location map of the study area is delineated from SEDAC and the topographical information is derived from Survey of India. Secondary data are collected from various published and unpublished sources.

Table 1: Details of Database

SENSOR		SATELLITE DATA	PATH/ROW	ACQUISITION DATE
LANDSAT	7	LANDSAT 7 IMAGERY	136/41	2003
ETM				
LANDSAT	8	LANDSAT 8 IMAGERY	136/41	2023
OLI/TIRS				

Source: USGS, Earth Explorer

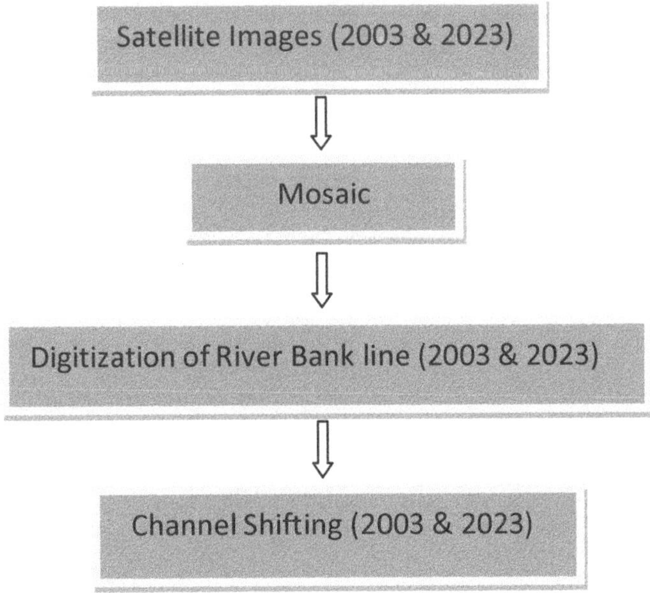

Figure 2. Flowchart for Bank line shifting

Results and Discussions

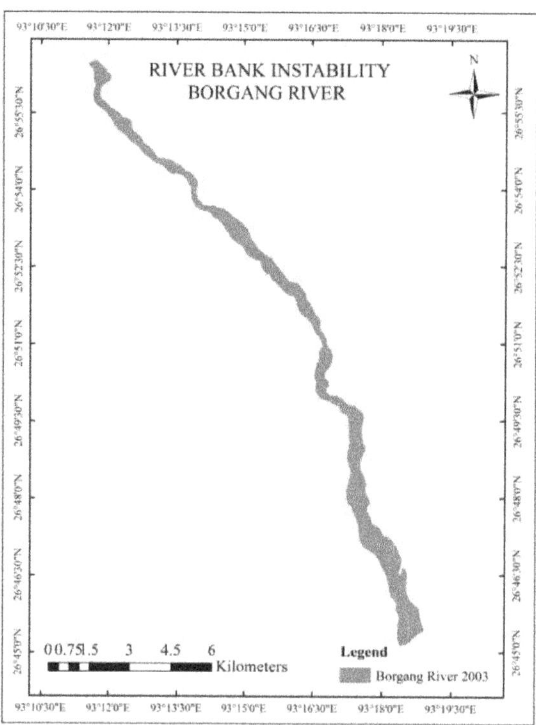

Figure 3. Channel Shifting of Borgang River, 2003

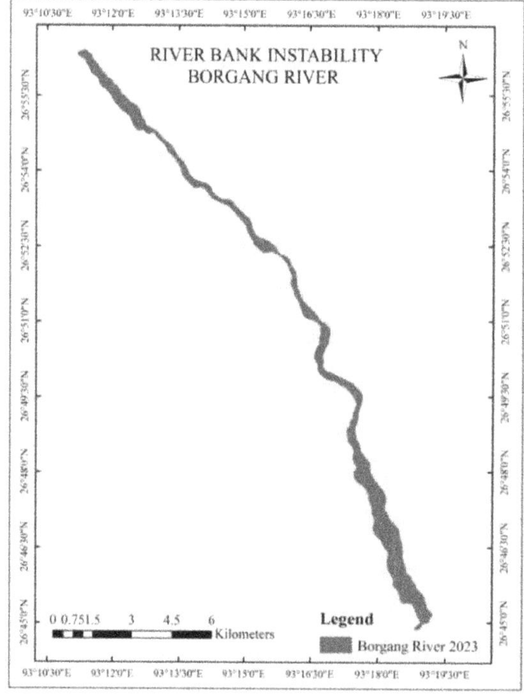

Figure 4. Channel Shifting of Borgang River, 2023

Shifting of Borgang River

Erosion is considered as a major concern in the district. Severe bank erosion in the district has been occurring since 2000 associated with the loss of land cover, households, and agricultural fields. Almost over 100 kilometers of distance area have been eroded in the study area and with this effect; hundreds of people have been displaced residing nearby the river banks. The satellite images for the year 2003 and 2023 have been prepared in order to analyze the shifting of the channel over a period of 20 years.

The above fig 3 & 4 represents the bank line shifting of Borgang River. The channel shifting of Borgang River is not uniform; some took place due to avulsion deposits and some others like geological structure, soil characteristics, tectonic activities, precipitation and anthropogenic influence.

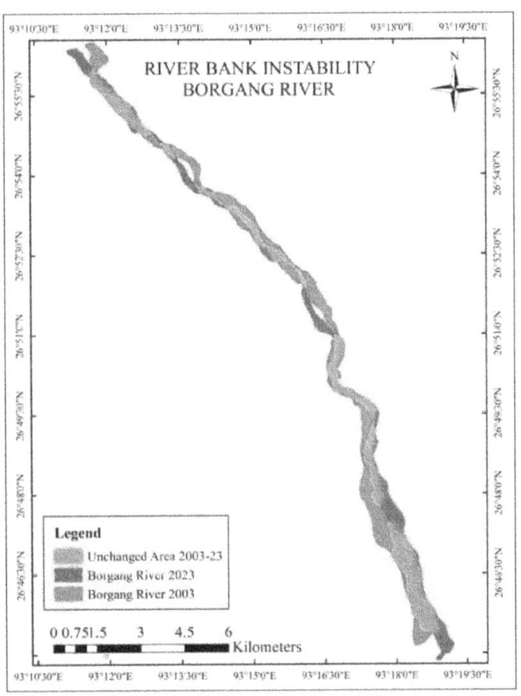

Figure 5. Channel Shifting of Borgang River, 2003-2023

The stability of the river bank is associated with the balance of the forces, resistivity of the river. The river bank instability of Borgang is frequent as the sediment transport is more and hence, the river equilibrium is lost. It is also characterized by the imbalance between erosive and depositional forces governed by the process of aggradations and depositional activities. From the above figures of 2003 and 2023, it can be seen that the river is meandering and the channel variability is low as compared to bank line changes in 2023. In some section of the river in the district, areas nearby the river side has been completely lost and mostly comes under high erosivity index.

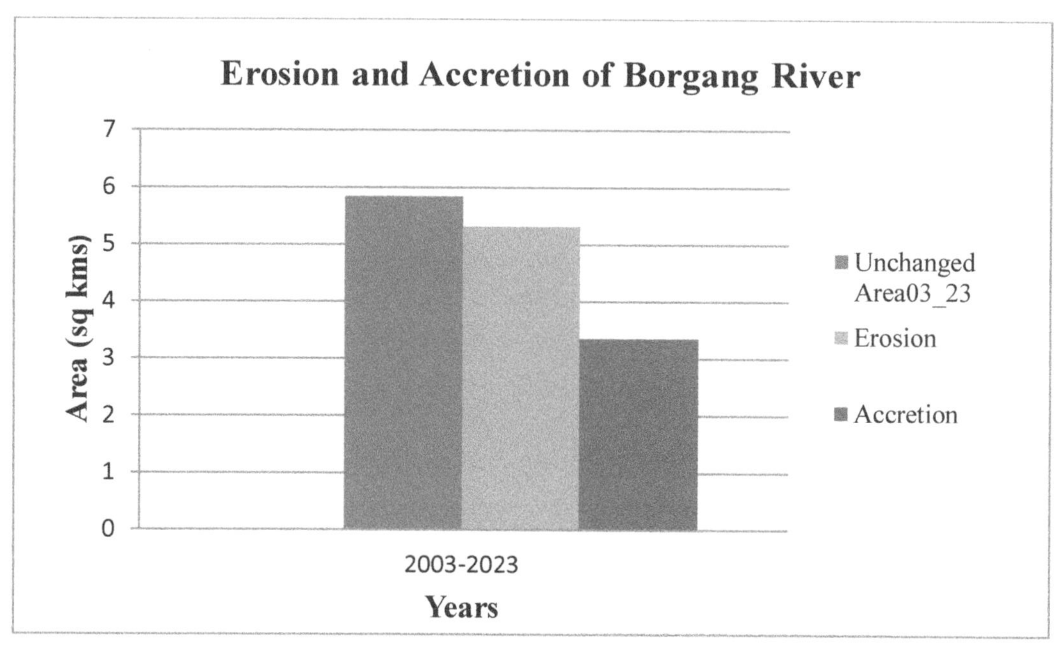

Figure 6. Erosion and Deposition of Borgang River 2003-2023

Biswanath circle in Biswanath district constitutes 357 villages. Out of these, 57 villages are mostly affected by flood/erosion activities by the river Brahmaputra and its tributaries Borgang, Buroi, Burigang. The nature and intensity of erosion depend upon the volume of water and garbages carried by these rivers. Besides these, it is very difficult to predict flash flood in the northern part of the circle as the rivers originating from Arunachal Pradesh carries huge amount of water causing widespread damage in the lower plains.

During 2003-2023, the river Borgang has eroded about 5.31 square kilometers of areas, whereas it has deposited about 3.35 square kilometers of areas. This signifies that the erosion rate of the river is maximum than the rate of deposition. As compared to 2023, the bank line change is strictly meandering where the channel variation is seen to be very high. The river has deposited huge amount of sediments leaving some areas under threat. About 5.84 square kilometers of areas has remained unchanged. The low lying areas in the extreme south of the river, Kathanibari part are facing the problem of acute erosion. Other villages Rangajan, Uriabasti, Birijan, and Gangmowthan are too vulnerable to erosion.

Conclusion

It is clear from the discussion that the river bank instability and its impact on settlement of Borgang River in Biswanath district are causing huge modifications in its landscape. The bank line shift of the channel directly and indirectly influences the rural dwellers making them homeless. The river receives sufficient amount of monsoon rainfall and it gets over flooded causing erosion mostly in its southern part. The proper planning and initiative measures are lagging behind though the government has invested its fund. Due to inappropriate measures, the local people residing in the riverside areas are still finding problem to survive. At any point of time they could be the victim bringing an untold misery and death.

References

Baishya J.Swarup (2013). "A Study on Bank Erosion by the River Baralia in Melkipara Village of Hajo Revenue Circle, Kamrup district, Assam, India." *International Journal of Scientific and Research Publications.* Vol.3, Issue 9: 1-10.

Basihya J.S. & Sahariah J.D., "Application of Remote Sensing and GIS for Flood Hazard Mapping: A Case study at Baralia-Nona River Basin, Assam, India." *International Journal of Humanities and Social Sciences.* Vol.5, issue 3, pp 58-70, 2017.

Chatterjee S., "Impact of River Bank Erosion on Human life: A case study in Shantipur Block, Noida District, and West Bengal." *International Journal of Humanities and Social Science Invention.*

Das K. Tuhin, Halder K. Sushil (2016)."River bank erosion induced human displacement and its consequences." Living Review of Landscape Research 8.3, pp: 1-35.

Dekaraja D. (2018). "Factors influencing migration in River Bank Eroded areas of Assam, India." Vol. 6, Issue 1.

Dutta N., Sonowal G., Thakuriah G. (2020). "A Study on the Bank Erosion by the River Jia Bharali and its impact on the Panchmile area of Tezpur town, Assam (India)." *International Journal of Advanced Research in Engineering and Technology,* 11(12), pp: 2358-2367.

Gogoi C. & Goswami C.D., (2013). "A Study on Bank Erosion and Bank line Migration pattern of the Subansiri river in Assam Using RS and GIS technology." *International Journal of Engineering and Science.* Vol. 2, Issue 9.

Guite L.T.S. & Bora A., (2016). "Impact of River Bank Erosion on Land cover in Lower Subansiri River Flood plain." *International Journal of Scientific and Research Publication.* Vol .6, Issue 5.

Lovric N. & Tosic R., (2016) "Assessment of Bank Erosion, Accretion and Channek shifting Using Remote sensing and GIS: A case study –Lower course of the Bosna River." Publication at https://www.researchgate.net/publication/303800552,

Sonowal G. and Dutta N. "River Bank Erosion in Rohmoria, Dibrugarh District part of Brahmaputra River, Assam (India) using Geospatial tools." Unpublished paper.

Statistical Handbook of Assam, 2021.

CHAPTER 13

Forest as Prospective of Eco – Tourism in Arunachal Pradesh

Naitik Kumar Biswas, Dipak Sharma, and Sailajananda Saikia

Abstract

Eco-Tourism is defined as "responsible travel to natural areas that conserves the environment, sustains the well-being of the local people, and involves interpretation and education" (TIES, 2015). Education is meant to be inclusive to both staff and guests.

Arunachal Pradesh is a picturesque mountainous region with high ridge lines and low-altitude foothills. The territory covers 83,743 km^2. Most of this land is hilly terrain, with a very small proportion of flat land covering about 4,450 km^2. The coordinates of Arunachal Pradesh are 28.2180°N Latitude and 94.7278°E Longitude. The physical background of Arunachal Pradesh is widely diverse with valleys, mountains, and hills with a dense network of rivers and rills, which broadens the scope for eco-tourism. Attractions of tourists who visit Arunachal are mainly constituting rich cultural practices of tribal communities, snow-clad mountains with scenic beauty, biodiversity, diverse cascading rivers, and now recently wildlife.

Through this paper, an attempt would be made on the eco-tourism model that focuses on conservation as much as it does on building the local economy. In 2021, the total forest and tree cover in India is 80.9 million hectares, which is 24.62% of the geographical area of the country. In Arunachal, the total forest cover is 79.33% of the Geographical area. The ISFR 2021 reports that 257 sq. km of forest cover was lost in Arunachal Pradesh. As a social support system, a forest can be utilized, ensuring that there should be no long-term damage to the forest & that it continues to provide resources.

Keywords: Conservation, Eco-Tourism, Forest, Local economy, SWOT Analysis,

Introduction

It is roughly estimated that the English-language word 'tourism' was 1st used in 1811. After 'The League of Nations' and 'United Nations' definitions of tourism, in 1941, Hunziker and Kraft defined tourism as "the sum of the phenomena and relationships arising from and stay of non-residents, insofar as they do not lead to permanent residence and are not connected with any earning activity". But in the present-day context, the tourism sector is utterly perceived as the business of providing services for people on holidays, for instance, transportation, hotels, restaurants, trips, etc... Tourism provides several fortuities to people who are remotely located. The region where the tourist is hosted procuresmultiple benefits out of services provided in the form of cash and other enlightening aspects. Tourism has become an important policy tool dedicated to change, development, and reconstruction of the physical and socio-cultural environments, and thus, as an industry, it defines and influences not only physical landscapes, land use, and planning but also social structures, local cultures and other (competing or collaborating) regional and local economies (Jarkko Saarinen er al., 2008).

The dizzy pace of life in cities often diverts the feeling of many towards nature, to get rid of from hustle and bustle of the city for a holiday. According to the United Nations World Tourism Organization (UNWTO) definition, ecotourism refers to all nature-based forms of tourism in which the main motivation of the tourists is the observation and appreciation of nature as well as the traditional cultures prevailing in natural areas. Eco-Tourism is a sub-component of the field of sustainable tourism. The model of ecotourism curtails the pessimistic impacts on the nature and socio-cultural environment. It also helps to generate income which benefits the host communities, institutions, organizations, and authorities economically which manage the natural areas. It strengthens awareness towards the sustention of nature and cultural assets, both among locals and tourists, and provides alternative opportunities for the local communities in terms of employment & income generation.

Among the types of tourism in India, ecotourism has grown recently. Ecotourism entails the sustainable preservation of a naturally endowed area or region. This is becoming more and more significant for the ecological development of all regions that have tourist value (Embassy for India, Riyadh). Among all the industries, tourism and Hospitality industry in India is one of the largest service industries. The total contribution of Travel & Tourism to the national economic output witnessed a much stronger growth of 43.6% in 2021 after the pandemic. With a contribution of 178.0 Bn USD, India ranked 6th in T&T's total contribution to GDP, in 2021 (Travel & Tourism Economic Impact 2022, WTTC).

Confederation of Indian Industry (CII), reports absolute annual direct contribution to travel and tourism to India's GDP was INR 9.25 trillion i.e. approximately US$ 125 billion in 2019, which indicates 3.3% of the country's GDP. However, due to Covid pandemic the industry was severely impacted. In 2021 foreign tourist arrival experienced a negative growth rate whereas the nation has witnessed 677.63 million domestic tourist visits. According to India Tourism statistic 2021, Arunachal experience at all time high tourist arrival in 2019 where 555639 domestic tourists and 7825 foreign tourist arrived in the state. Conforming to a report published in The Arunachal Times it was estimated that if there would be no pandemic the number of tourist visit would cross 6 Lakhs mark subsequently in the report it was also estimated the total loss of income from tourism to the state was near about 142 crore, which is 0.91% of the gross state value added because of pandemic.

Study Region

Arunachal Pradesh 'Land of Dawn-Lit Mountains' is situated in the North-Eastern Region of India. It is also known as the Land of Rising Sun because this is where the sun rises first in India. Till 1972, it was known as the North-Eastern Frontier Agency (NEFA). It gained the Union Territory status on January 20, 1972, and was renamed 'Arunachal Pradesh' by Bibhabasu Das Shastri, the Director of Research, and K.A.A. Raja, then Chief Commissioner of Arunachal Pradesh. The state earned a full-fledged state status on February 20, 1987. The area of the state is 83,743 sq km and the region lies roughly between 91.20° to 97.30° East longitude and 26.28° to 29.30° North latitude. Arunachal shares a long international border with 3 Nations namely, Bhutan which is in the west (160 km), China in the north and northeast part (1,080 km), and Myanmar in the eastern side (440 km). Area wise it is the largest state in the Northeastern region and the least densely populated state in India.

Arunachal is a land of lush green forests, snow-capped mountains, deep river valleys, and diverse tribal groups. It has extensive geographical diversity and climatic conditions varying from tropical to temperate and alpine with a variety of wildlife, flora, and fauna. The area is mostly mountainous with Himalayan ranges along the northern borders crisscrossed with mountain ranges running north-south. There are five river valleys in the state: the Kameng, the Subansiri, the Siang, the Lohit, and the Tirap. Except for Tirap which is fed by the Patkai Range the rest of the rivers and rivulets in the state are fed by glaciers in the Himalayas. Among the rivers, the ferocious is the Siang, known as Tsangpo in Tibet. The mountain ranges, dense forests, and rivers have prevented interconnection between tribes.

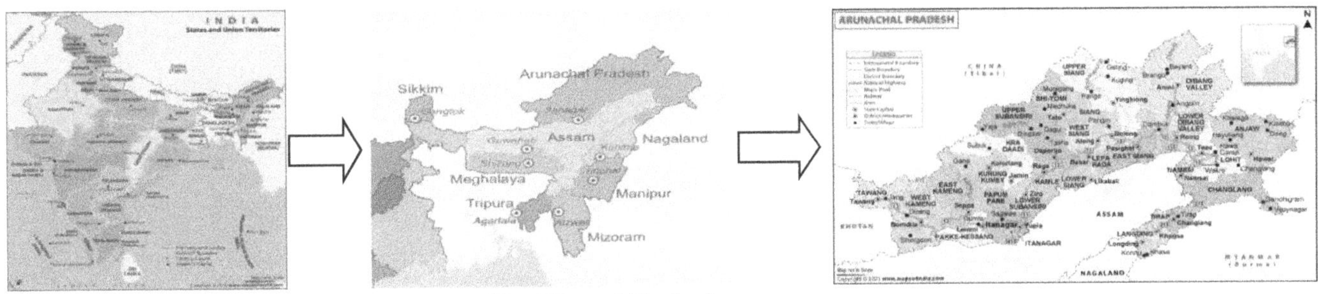

Fig. Map of Study Area
Source: www.mapsofindia.com

Objective

The basic objective of the current study is to examine the impact of Community Participation in Sustainable Tourism Development regarding forests as Eco-Tourism sites in Arunachal Pradesh. The major objectives of this research work are as follows:

1. To site the prospective of Eco-Tourism in Arunachal Pradesh.
2. Create a model for conservation to show that conservation pays for the local economy.

Database and Methodology

The study is descriptive type basically on data from secondary sources. The data from secondary sources are collected from books, journals, articles, research papers, websites, and especially fromMinistry of Tourism Government of India, Arunachal Pradesh Tourism Department, Indian State of Forest Report and Department of Environment and Forest, Arunachal Pradesh.

The different materials collected from various sources especially websites have been interpreted logically and systematically under appropriate headings in such a way as to get the results. SWOT Analysis was used to draw a meaningful conclusion.

Result and Discussion

Overview of Forestry Scenario

Arunachal Pradesh is a forest-rich state in the Eastern Himalayan region in North Eastern Region of India. As per the Champion & Seth Classification (1968), the forests in Arunachal Pradesh belong to 11 Type Groups which are further divided into 23 different Forest Types (India State of Forest Report 2019). The state has about 20% species of the country's fauna, about 4,500 species of flowering plants, 400 species of pteridophytes, 23 species of conifers, 35 species of bamboos, 20 species of canes, 52 species of Rhododendron and more than 500 species of orchids. Cane and bamboo are found in abundance. As of India's State of Forest Report, 2019, the state has 51,407 sq km of Recorded Forest Area (RFA) out of which 10,589 sq km is Reserved Forest, 9779 sq km is Protected Forest and 31,039 sq km is Unclassed Forest.

In local communities' forests are the linchpin of the economy and livelihoods. From prehistoric time the tribal people of the state have been closely associated with and deliberately depending on forest resources. Although, the increase in population, developing activities, and practices like shifting cultivation, the pressure on forest resources is invariably increasing, leading to their degradation and affecting rejuvenation and productivity. Tropical rainforests are found in the foothills and hilly terrain down the eastern side of the Myanmar border and Alpine forests are mostly found in the Northern part of the state. "The diversity of topographical and climatic conditions has favored the growth of luxuriant forests, which are home to myriad plant and animal forms, adding beauty to the landscape (arunachalforests.nic.in)".

Forest cover in the state

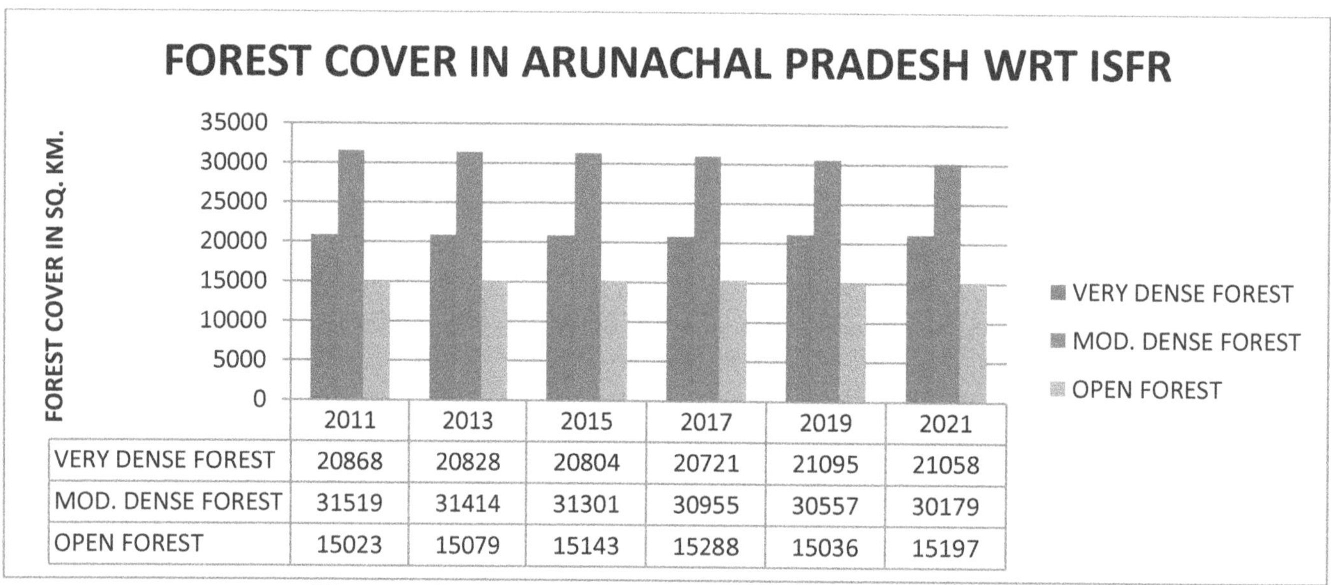

	2011	2013	2015	2017	2019	2021
VERY DENSE FOREST	20868	20828	20804	20721	21095	21058
MOD. DENSE FOREST	31519	31414	31301	30955	30557	30179
OPEN FOREST	15023	15079	15143	15288	15036	15197

Figure: - Forest cover in Arunachal Pradesh WRT ISFR
Source: - India state of Forest Report (ISFR)

Pursuant to interpreted data of indigenous LISS-III sensor of IRS Resource sat series of satellites in the period of Oct to Dec 2019, the Forest Cover in the State is 66,431 sq km which is 79.33% of the State's total geographical area, as per 2021 Indian State of Forest Report (ISFR). Classification of the forest cover in the state is done based on tree canopy density into pre-defined classes, viz., very dense forest (VDF), moderately dense forest (MDF), and open forest (OF).Land with tree canopy density 0f 70% and above is known as Very Dense Forest, 40% and more but less than 70% is known as

Moderately Dense Forest and 10% and more but less than 40 % is categories as Open Forest. Concerning the forest canopy density classes, the state has 21058 sq km of Very Dense Forest (VDF), 30,179 sq km of Moderately Dense Forest (MDF), and 15,197 sq km under Open Forest (OF). Forest cover in the state has decreased by 257 sq km as compared to the previous assessment report of ISFR 2019.

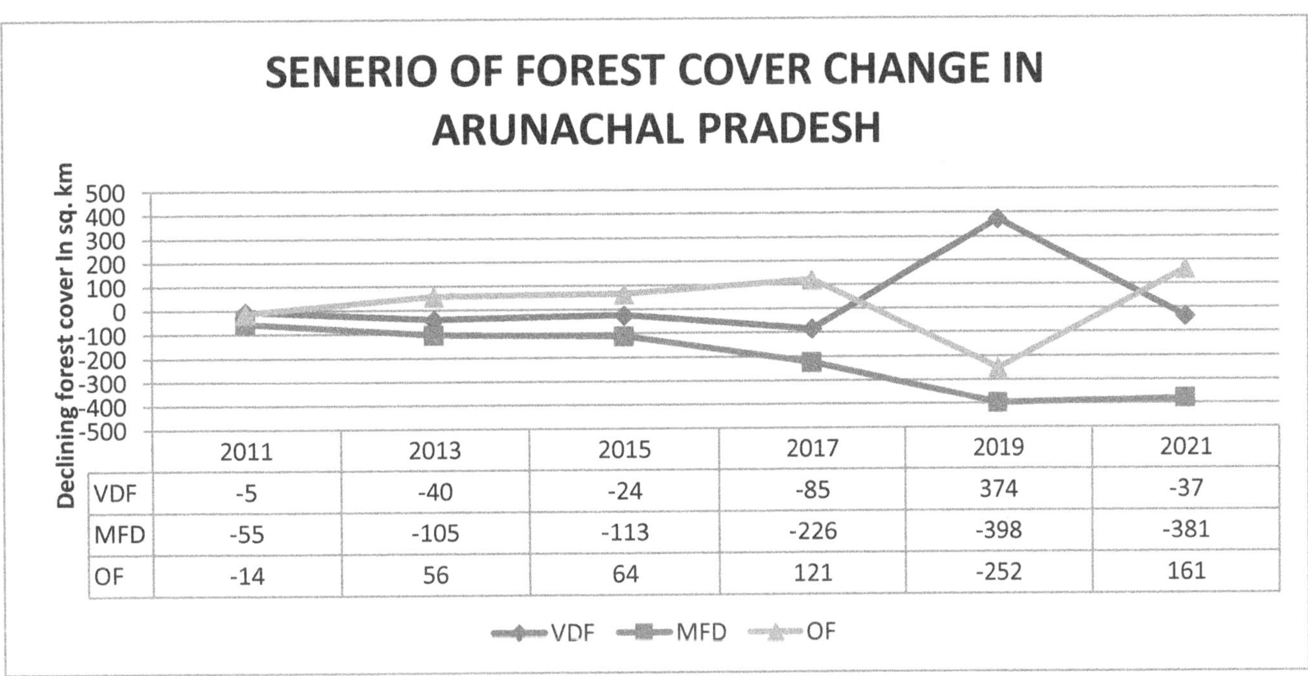

	2011	2013	2015	2017	2019	2021
VDF	-5	-40	-24	-85	374	-37
MFD	-55	-105	-113	-226	-398	-381
OF	-14	56	64	121	-252	161

Figure: - Forest cover change in Arunachal Pradesh
Source: - India state of Forest Report (ISFR)

The forest of the state is also exposed to number of problems which menace their prosperities. Many of the problems are man made out of which in trend are deforestation, traditional agricultural practices (jhuming), mining, illegal logging, constructions, encroachment, illegal wildlife smuggles. The problems has led to loss of forest cover, split of forests, loss of habitat for wildlife, a negative impact on biodiversity, degradation of ecosystem services, etc... Forest fires and Climate change are another two factors which hampers the forest of the region. Some areas are also vulnerable due to forest fire, which can be caused by both natural and human. Climate change has its diverse impact. Temperature and Precipitation anomaly due to climate change can create difference in configuration and distribution of forest species.

Forest creating prospects of Eco-Tourism in Arunachal Pradesh

Eco-Tourism in Arunachal Pradesh is auspicious sector, as its forests serve a great prospective for sustainable tourism. It is located in the Eastern Himalayan ranges of North East Region and is the most picturesque tourist destination in India. There is tremendous potential for the growth of tourism in Arunachal Pradesh; especially, eco-tourism and adventure tourism. Tourists who visit here can also learn about the traditional local lifestyles and prevailing cultures of local communities who have been residing in polyphony with their local environment for generations. As of now there are 14 tourist circuits in the state. Each circuit gives a different experience to the visitor as the circuits are unique from one another in terms of location and cultural diversity.

Arunachal is home to a number of protected areas, including 9 wildlife sanctuaries, 2 National parks, and 1 biosphere reserves, with their lush green tropical forests teeming with wildlife. Some of the popular protected areas in the state are Mouling National Park, Namdapha National Park,Eaglenest wildlife sanctuary,Kamlang Wildlife Sanctuary & Tiger Reserve, Pakke Tiger Reserve, Dibang Wildlife Sanctuary, etc... Forest of the state is home to a diverse range of species i.e. more than 500 in number, and is home to four major cats namely tiger, leopard, clouded leopard, snow leopard and also rare lesser feline species like Golden Cat and Marbled Cat.The Dihang-Dibang biosphere reserve is spread out in 3 districts of state namely: Dibang Valley, Upper Siang and West Siang. It is one of the largest biosphere reserves in the country. The Mouling National Park and the Dibang Wildlife Sanctuary are located utterly within the premises of this biosphere reserve. The reserve is home to several flora and fauna species; it has around 500 species of plants, more than 60 species of mammals, and number of different birds. In addition to the protected area, the state has numbers of reserve forest and community-based forest which provides prospect for Eco-Tourism in the state. Tourists can experience a variety of nature-based activities, such as trekking, hiking, camping, bird watching, wildlife watching and educational walk.

Conservation of the forest & Its Importance

Forest conservation is the practice of planting and maintaining forested area for the benefit and sustainability of future generations (K.v. Pawar, Ravi V. Rathkar). It is the practice of protecting forest resources for benefits of Mother Nature, wild animals and ultimately mankind. Conservation practice is important because the forest plays a vital role in preserving global biodiversity, governing the Earth's climate, offering clean air and water, and assisting with human survival and traditional knowledge. As a social support system forest should not be completely closed and never kept as unutilized but forest should be used ensuring that there should not be long term damage to the forest (Dr. Sejal Worah, WWF India).

In India Jabarkhet Natural Reserve (JNR) located in Uttarakhand is the best example of forest conservation and promotion of Eco-Tourism through forest. It is growing as a popular tourist destination for the wildlife enthusiast and nature lover who come to explore the natural beauty of the region. The model of the tourism in JNRinvolves developing of tourism infrastructure in a manner that is ecologically sound and socially ethical. In addition, the model also gives importance to the involvement of local communities in the Eco-tourism industry and boosting the local economy by providing different job opportunity. The locals have also set up many business facilities in the vicinity of the reserve. The reserve being a privately owned natural reserve achieved tremendous heights on sustainable tourism model.

The Eaglenest wildlife sanctuaryis located in the West Kameng District of Arunachal pradesh, it is home to over 600 species of birds. Bugun tribe is one of the smallest tribes of Arunachal Pradesh who resides in the vicinity of the sanctuary. Bugun communities stopped hunting and logging and joined in the efforts to the conserve the sanctuary. The conservation model involves the active participation of the local communities in conservation effort. The feeling of ownership among the communities came after when the bird species was named after the tribe's name which is BugunLoicichla. The bird species worldwide is only found in the Eaglenest Sanctuary. In 2017 the Bugun Community decleared over 17 sq. km of thcir land as thc Sinchung Village Community Reserve. It acts as a buffer to the core area of the Eagle nest wildlife reserve. For their efforts they were awarded the India Biodiversity Award 2018 in the conservation of wildlife species category, conferred by the National Biodiversity Authority. Many tourists visit the sanctuary for nature walk, educational walk & for bird watching purposes. The rise of tourism in the place is boosting economy of the Bugun Tribe in the region.

Analysis

The state of Arunachal Pradesh has tremendous scope for tourism. The envelope of tourism sector in the state is not unfurled in a proper way. Tourism can be a key economic drive for the state, at the same time it is essential to ensure sustainable and diligent tourism development that should benefit the host communities and safeguards the regions natural and cultural legacy. State's forests and Eco-tourism are closely linked with each other, forest of the state sheltering a diverse range of flora and fauna. The forest cover of the state is more than 60% i.e. 79.33% of the State's total geographical area, as per 2021ISFR, making it one of the plentiful biodiversity hotspots in the planet earth. Eco-Tourism in Arunachal Pradesh circles around the forests; it offers the tourists distinctive possibilities to enjoy the natural beauty of the region while promoting conservation efforts. The regions are also home to abundant medicinal plants which promotes the educational eco-tourism in the state. Some of the scarcely-seen and endangered species, including the clouded leopard, Himalayan snow-leopard, Red Panda, flying Squirrel andBugunLoicichla ; holds the potential to entice many tourist in the region. The tribal peoples who are engaged in illegal logging, hunting and other unlawful activities can be enlightened by Eco-Tourism as it will prove alternative sources of income for local communities, and subsequently it will reduce the pressure on the forest.

The data of Arunachal Forest Cover by ISFR displays that the Moderate Dense Forest is in high proportion in the state and it is declining consistently over time. Subsequently Very Dense Forest of the state is also decreasing, other than the data of 2019 where the canopy class experienced a sharp increase. It can be seen that the density of the forest in the state is decreasing and biennially data of Open Forest cover is Increasing, it a matter of concern from not only the view of hampering the Eco-Tourism model but also it will create havoc for the wildlife's, which will ultimately led to Human Animal Conflict.

Despite having so much of potential for tourism in the state, the state of Arunachal Pradesh has gained so less from it. Arunachal got status of full-fledged state in 1987 and its first "Tourism Policy" drafted in March 2003 i.e. after 14 years. The framework for the development of Tourism in Arunachal and preparation of 20 years perspective Plan for the state was made. After completion of 20 years, still the state is facing with a large number of problems in promoting tourism in the state. Regardless of problems some sort of tourism development was seen in recent years. Yet there is no any separate & strong policy to promote Eco-tourism in the state, which keeps the potential to become the backbone of the state's economy. The state government should also release its own state's tourism statistics in line with the Indian tourism statistics for better policy making for the Tourism sector.

SWOT Analysis

STRENGTHS
- o Diverse range of flora and fauna in thestate generates a unique and thrilling experience for eco-tourism.
- o The distinct culture of the diverse indigenous tribes prevailing in the state attracts a number of tourists.
- o Arunachal is comparatively untouched by newfangled development, which can attract the tourist seeking for virgin natural environment.

o The state has several options for adventure tourism such as river rafting, paragliding, MTB, trekking, mountaineering, wildlife safaris, etc… which has the potential for attracting the adventure seeking tourist.

WEAKNESS

o Less number of infrastructural developments in the remote locations hinders the tourist to visit the places.

o The state has limited transportation link making it challenging to travel within the state.

o Many people of the mainland India and abroad India are unaware of the potential of Eco-Tourism in the state.

o The state is lacking in social development, mostly in the rural areas.

OPPORTUNITIES

- Global trend towards eco-system displays notable chances for the state.
- The model of eco-tourism will increase the local economy that will encourage the peoples to conserve forest.
- National parks and Wildlife Sanctuary in the state creates an opportunity for the Eco-Tourist.
- Community based reserve forest in the state can attract a large sort of tourists.
- Eco tourism can help in Eco-restoration of the environment.

THREATS

- If the proposed sector does not manage properly, it could lead to environmental degradation as because of increase in tourist. It could also hurt the nature and cultural assets of the region
- Climate change is the main threat, as the temperature and annual rainfall anomaly continues it gives a negative impact on the region's natural resources and settings.
- It is threatened by limitation of its potential market as the state faces competition from other destinations that offers similar eco-tourism experience, such as Assam and Meghalaya.
- Insurgency and political conflicts also hinder the prospect of the state to flourish as tourism hub.

Conclusion

Overall, the state's natural environment, unique wildlife, rivers, rills, mountains and forest makes it's an unmissable destination for tourism. The forest of the state provides a great potential for Eco-Tourism. The sector can contribute to the conservation of state's rich biodiversity and provides employment opportunities for the local communities.

However, the state has a high forest cover making it an important resource for the state as well as for the country. The forest has also threats, including illegal logging, encroachment, and illegal hunting's. Over time the Arunachal government has taken certain steps to protect its rich forests, by implementing definite regulations and by supporting sustainable forest management practices. There should be social contract with the communities to aware them for using the forest in a sensible or sustainable manner. The forest of the state has experienceda declining trend in the recent days as because the population of the state is also rising in a rapid manner and creating a pressure on the forest and its resources. This is due to the region that the state accommodates a large number of tribal communities which are mostly dependent on the forest from time immemorial.

Both Jabarkhet Natural Reserve and Bugun Community Forest avoids mass tourism gathering, for conserving it from distortion and for not exerting pressure on the forest. As a social support system, the forest should be utilized, ensuring that there should be no long-term damage to the forest and that it continues to provide resources and livelihood the people. At the end of the day a thriving forest with wildlife is going to bring economic benefits but cutting the tress is going to bring temporary economic benefits. Preserving the forest and conserving it and getting people visit in the forest and paying to come can be a good initiative to earn a larger term of economic benefits.

By utilizing its strengths and addressing its weakness and threats, the state of Arunachal Pradesh can be a leading Eco-Tourism hub, contributing to the state's economic developing while securing the natural and cultural heritage for future generation.

References

Chhetri, B and Lal, U(2017): "Impact of Tourism on traditional livelihood in Lachung valley of Sikkim Himalaya".The Deccan Geographer, Vol. 55, No. 1 & 2, June and December, 2017, pp. 66-75.

Debnath J., et al.(2020-2021): "Strategy for maintain environmental quality through identification of potential areas for afforestation: A case study from North-East India". North Eastern Geographer, Vol. 41, No. 1 & 2, pp. 3-21.

Doughlas, G.P. (1999): "Contemporary Issues in Tourist Development" New York, Routledge Publication.

Saarinen J. (2008):"Tourism as a Sustainable Development Factor, Botswana Notes and Records" Botswana Society Vol. 39, pp. 43-53.

Taher, M and Ahmed P. (2017): "Geography of North-East India, Mani Manik Prakash Publications, Guwahati.

Lama, M. (2020): "Arunachal loses 2.02 lakh tourisr arrivals due to Covid-19 lockdown". The Arunachal Times publication, Itanagar.

Indian Tourism Department(2003): "Project 20 years Perspective (Tourism) Plan for the State of Arunachal Pradesh".

Indian State of Forest Report (2011, 2013, 2015, 2017, 2019, 2021): "Forest Survey of India".

Mandal Ram K., et al. (2021): "Eco-Tourism Industry in Arunachal Pradesh: An Empirical Study". Turkish Online Journal of Qualitative Inquiry, Vol. 12, Issued 6, 2021.

Pawar, K. V&Rothkar Ravi K (2015): "Forest Conservation & Environmental Awareness". Global Challenges, Policy Framework & Sustainable Development for Mining of Mineral and Fossil Energy Resources (GCPF 2015).

Omo, P (2020): "Potential and Prospective of Tourism in Arunachal Pradesh: A Geographical Analysis". Doctoral dissertation, Rajiv Gandhi University.

Department of Forest (2017): "Forest Statistics of Arunachal Pradesh".

Sandeepa and Chetan (2019): "Indidejabarkhet: One of India's rare privately-owned nature reserves has much to teach about eco conservation". Firstpost Publication.

Eco India (2020): "An eco-tourism model that focuses on forest conservation and building the local economy". Scroll Publication.

Agarwala, T (2018): " How Arunachal Pradesh's Bugun tribe won a national conservation award". Indian Express Publication.

Paljor, K (2022): "Watch: How Arunachal's Bugun tribals protect a wildlife sanctuary". East Mojo Publication.

Tayeng, M (2020): "Geographical analysis on prospects of adventure tourism in Arunachal Pradesh". Doctoral dissertation, Rajiv Gandhi University.